Feminist Theologies
Legacy and Prospect

ROSEMARY RADFORD RUETHER
Editor

FORTRESS PRESS
MINNEAPOLIS

FEMINIST THEOLOGIES
Legacy and Prospect

A similar version of N. Tohidi's piece has appeared in the following volume: *The Blackwell Companion to Contemporary Islamic Thought*, Ibrahim M. Abu-Rabi, ed. (Oxford, UK/ Malden, MA: Blackwell Publishing, 2006).

Cover image: *Four Women* by Jane Sterrett, copyright © Images.com / CORBIS. Used by permission.
Cover design: Kevin van der Leek Design
Interior design: Michelle Norstad and Timothy W. Larson
This book was typeset using Adobe Perpetua.

Library of Congress Cataloging-in-Publication Data
Feminist theologies : legacy and prospect / Rosemary Radford Ruether, editor.
  p. cm.
 ISBN-13: 978–0–8006–3894–8 (alk. paper)
 ISBN-10: 0–8006–3894–8 (alk. paper)
 1. Feminist theology. I. Ruether, Rosemary Radford.
BT83.55.F448 2007
230.082—dc22   2006034701

Manufactured in the U.S.A.

11   10   09   08   07   2   3   4   5   6   7   8   9   10

Contents

CONTENTS

Contributors

Rita Nakashima Brock. Visiting scholar, Starr King School of Ministry, Berkeley, California. One of the founders of Asian-American Women in Theology and Ministry. Author of *Journeys by Heart: A Christology of Erotic Power* (1988); *Setting the Table: Women in Theological Conversation* (with Claudia Camp and Serene Jones) (1995); *Casting Stones: Prostitution and Liberation in Asia and the U.S.* (with Susan Thistlethwaite) (1996); and *Proverbs of Ashes: Violence, Redemptive Suffering and the Search for What Saves Us* (with Rebecca Parker) (2001).

Sandy Boucher. Recipient "Outstanding Woman in Buddhism" award, United Nations, 2006. Author of *Turning the Wheel: American Women Creating the New Buddhism* (1988, 1993); *Opening the Lotus: A Woman's Guide to Buddhism* (1997); *Discovering KwanYin: Buddhist Goddess of Compassion* (1999); *Hidden Spring: A Buddhist Woman Confronts Cancer* (2000); and *Dancing in the Dharma: The Life and Teachings of Ruth Denison* (2005).

Peggy Cleveland. After serving as codirector for the Center for Women and Religion, Berkeley, California, Peggy moved to Mendocino County to develop an organic vegetable and flower farm, teach Philosophy and Women as Writers at Mendocino Community College, and direct a federally funded program for retired senior volunteers. In 1992 she moved to Cabarrus County, North Carolina, to become executive director of Cabarrus Cooperative Christian Ministry. She retired in 1996.

Pamela Cooper-White. Former director of the Center for Women and Religion, Berkeley, California. Presently Professor of Pastoral Theology, Lutheran Theological Seminary, Philadelphia. Author of *Cry of Tamar: Violence against Women and the Church's Response* (1995), *Shared Wisdom: Use of the Self in Pastoral Care and Counseling* (2003), and *Many Voices: Pastoral Psychotherapy in Relational and Theological Perspective* (2006).

Marcia Falk. Pioneering Jewish feminist scholar, poet, and translator. In addition to three books of poetry, she has published a bilingual re-creation of Jewish liturgy in poetic forms, *The Book of Blessings* (1996). Her translations include *The Song of Songs: Love Lyrics from the Bible* (2004); *The Spectacular Difference*, poems by the twentieth-century Hebrew mystic Zelda (2004); and *With Teeth in the Earth,* poems of the Yiddish modernist Malka Heifetz Tussman (1992). A professor of literature and creative writing for fifteen years at SUNY Binghamton, the Claremont Colleges, and Stanford, she is now an Affiliated Scholar at the Graduate Theological Seminary in Berkeley, California, and lectures on Jewish women's poetry and other topics.

Mary E. Hunt. Cofounder of WATER (Women's Alliance for Theology, Ethics and Ritual), Silver Springs, Maryland. Author of *Fierce Tenderness: A Feminist Theology of Friendship* (1991) and *Good Sex: Feminist Perspectives from the World's Religions* (2001).

Cheryl A. Kirk-Duggan. Former director of the Center for Women and Religion, Berkeley, California. Presently Professor of Theology and Women's Studies, Shaw Divinity School, Raleigh, North Carolina. Author and editor of twenty-two books, her work includes: *Violence and Theology* (2006); *The Sky Is Crying: Race, Class, and Natural Disaster* (2006) (editor), a response to Hurricane Katrina; *Soul Pearls: Worship Resources for the Black*

Church (2003); *Misbegotten Anquish: A Theology and Ethics of Violence* (2001); *Undivided Soul: Helping Connect Body and Spirit* (2001); *Refiner's Fire: A Religious Engagement with Violence* (2001); and *Exorcising Evil: A Womanist Perspective on the Spirituals* (1997).

Stephanie Mitchem. Former Professor of Theology, University of Detroit, Mercy College. Presently Professor of Religious Studies, University of South Carolina. Author of *Introducing Womanist Theology* (2001).

Nancy Pineda-Madrid. Professor of Theology, Boston College. Author of numerous articles on Latina feminist theology, such as "Chicana Feminist Epistemology," in *A Reader in Latina Feminsit Theology*, ed. Maria Pilar Aquino (2002), 241–266; and "Traditioning: The Formation of Community, the Transmission of Faith," in *Futuring Our Past: Explorations in the Theology of Tradition*, ed. Orlando Espín and Gary Macy (2006), 204–226.

Rosemary Radford Ruether. Carpenter Professor of Feminist Theology, Berkeley, California. Emerita, presently visiting scholar, Claremont Graduate University and Claremont School of Theology, Claremont, California. Author or editor of forty-two books, most recently *Integrating Ecofeminism, Globalization and World Religions* (2005) and *Goddess and the Divine Feminine: A Western Religious History* (2005).

Nayereh Tohidi. Professor of Women's Studies in Religion, State University of California, Northridge, and research associate, UCLA, in Middle Eastern Studies. Author or editor of six major books, among them *Women in Muslim Societies: Diversity in Unity* (1998) and *Globalization, Gender and Religion: The Politics of Women's Rights in Muslim and Catholic Contexts* (with Jane Bayes) (2001).

Mary Evelyn Tucker. Professor of Religion, Bucknell University; organizer of twelve conferences on ecology and world religions through the Center for World Religions, Harvard Divinity School; codirector of the Forum on Religion and Ecology; author or editor of numerous books on religion and ecology, among them *Worldly Wonder: Religions Enter Their Ecological Phrase* (2003) and *World Views and Ecology* (with John Grim) (1994).

Introduction

Rosemary Radford Ruether

THE CHAPTERS IN THIS VOLUME were originally presentations given at a day-long conference at the Graduate Theological Union (GTU) in Berkeley, California, on March 30, 2005, to celebrate the history and work of the Center for Women and Religion at the GTU.[1] The Center for Women and Religion (CWR) was perhaps the first important center of women and religion at a major seminary or consortium of seminaries in the United States (or anywhere). It was opened as the Office of Women's Affairs in 1970 and provided stellar leadership in promoting women's presence as faculty and students, support for women, and the development of feminist studies in religion over its almost thirty-five years of existence. This book's first chapter, "The History of the Center for Women and Religion," captures some of the highlights of this history at the GTU, 1970–2003.

Five former CWR staff, directors, and codirectors, Peggy Cleveland, Mary Cross, Barbara Waugh, Pamela Cooper-White, and Cheryl Kirk-Duggan, shared some reminiscences of that history. Three of these reflections are included as part of the first chapter: "Reflections on the Early Years at CWR," by Peggy Cleveland; "The Early 1990s: Whose CWR? Whose Feminism?" by Pamela Cooper-White; and "Dreams, Visions, and Disconnects," by Cheryl Kirk-Duggan. The conference also wanted to make very clear that this history has not come to an end. Indeed, it is more important than ever at this moment in time to renew the work of feminist critique of religion and its many cultural, political, and economic ramifications. A group of GTU women faculty launched a new program in the fall of 2006. This program's focus is more strictly academic than that of the former CWR; it has been shaped to maintain the feminist critique and revisioning of religion at the GTU. As a certificate program in women's studies in religion, it draws broadly on faculty across all of the GTU schools and can be a first or second major within a master's or doctoral program in any field of study.

The Women's Studies in Religion Program describes its purpose in this way:

> In an effort to sustain, promote and advance the commitment to the study of women and religion in full recognition of experiences of race, sexual and gender orientation, ethnicity, class, culture, nationality and religious orientation at the Graduate Theological Union, we propose to create a Program for Women's Studies in Religion (WSR Program), the goals of which would be:
>
> 1. To enhance the academic offerings available to students throughout the GTU by providing a rigorous and interdisciplinary certificate program in the study of women and religion.
> 2. To host colloquium series, workshops, symposia or conferences (as permitted by personnel and resources) to support research and exchanges in the study of women and religion.
> 3. To support and encourage new initiatives in women's studies by interested faculty and students.
> 4. To formalize the GTU's links with the Gender Consortium at the University of California at Berkeley.

The establishment of this Women's Studies in Religion Program affirms the GTU's long-standing commitment to women's studies in theology and religion; builds upon the network of academic and community centers and initiatives that have been established at or in relation to the GTU for the study and support of women in religion; and recognizes the innovative work contributed by consortial women faculty in the theological and religious disciplines. With a strong academic thrust, the WSR Program will serve Master's (MA, MDiv, MTS) and Doctoral students (PhD and DMin) who desire to concentrate on women's studies in their degree program. A "WSR Certificate" and a "Colloquium Series" will be the main programmatic strands.

The third important item on the agenda of the conference was to introduce something of the enormously creative diversity of feminist or women-centered theologies that have developed in the last thirty-five years. When Clare Fischer (presently emerita professor of social ethics at Starr King School for the Ministry) first set out to compile bibliographies on women and religion back in 1975, the pickings were slim indeed, although not nonexistent. Today, thirty-five years later, the development of feminist reflection in every field of religious studies, such as scripture, theology, church history, pastoral psychology, and ethics, has proliferated in the Christian world. Feminist studies in religion have also developed across world religions—Judaism, Islam, and Buddhism, among others. Feminist theology and critique are situating themselves across ethnic and cultural contexts: African American women choose to call themselves womanists or black feminists; Latinas call themselves Latina feminists or *mujeristas*; Asian Americans and many other affinity groups, particularly lesbian feminists, are making their own reflections related to their own community and historical experiences.

The intention of the conference was to lift up a small sample of this enriching diversification across religious and cultural-ethnic-sexual lines. Authors of four of this book's chapters in Part Two write from different contexts within Christianity to discuss how they understand feminist theology and its contribution to an educational institution such as the GTU. Rita Nakashima Brock writes from an Asian American perspective, Mary Hunt from a lesbian liberation perspective, Stephanie

Mitchem from an African American woman's or womanist perspective, and Nancy Pineda-Madrid from a Latina feminist viewpoint. The next group of four essays features perspectives from Buddhism, Judaism, and Islam. Sandy Boucher writes from a Buddhist feminist view, Nayereh Tohidi from a Muslim perspective, and Mary Evelyn Tucker from the perspective of world religions and ecology. Liturgist and poet Marcia Falk's essay focuses on poetry and prayer in the Jewish tradition.

These papers provide only a sample of the rich diversity of feminist religious perspectives that have developed in the last several decades. Since this was only a one-day conference, we decided to limit ourselves to the diversity within the United States. But feminist theology is expanding today not only across religious and cultural communities but across every continent. Lively feminist theologies are being developed in Asia, Latin America, Europe, Africa, and the Middle East, from many religious perspectives. But to give adequate attention to that enormous wealth would take a much longer conference and a much bigger book. We have augmented this work with select bibliographies in the particular contexts discussed in the chapters.

Part One

Women at the Center

CHAPTER ONE

The History of the Center for Women and Religion

Rosemary Radford Ruether

THE CENTER FOR WOMEN AND RELIGION (CWR) at the Graduate Theological Union in Berkeley, California, began as the Office of Women's Affairs (OWA) in 1970.[1] At first an associated institution, it was accepted after four years as a sponsored center of the GTU. The OWA, later CWR, began with a multidimensional vision of its role as a place of support for all women at the GTU: students, faculty, staff, and female spouses of male faculty and students. Among its early programs, services, and activities in the first five years were a small circulating library of books and literature on women (named for Anne McGrew Bennett); a place for consciousness-raising groups; a place for meetings of its own board of directors and for local church task forces on women; classes and craft workshops; and special programs.

The OWA/CWR promoted research on women; changes in the curriculum to include women's issues in all fields of theological education; an increase in the number female students, faculty, and administrators; vocational and psychological counseling for women; outreach to women pastors and task forces in local churches; and networking with women's organizations and women and religion groups nationally, such as the National Organization of Women, the University of California at Berkeley Center for Continuing Education of Women, women's health collectives, Bay Area abortion clinics, and the Women's Caucus of the American Academy of Religion.

One of the courses held in the fall of 1971 and offered to all students throughout the GTU was called "Women in Ministry: Toward a Whole Theology." The coordinator of the course was an activist from San Francisco State University, Sally Gearhart. Three "wise women from the East" were invited to give three sessions each over a weekend once a month. They were Peggy Way of the Divinity School of the University of Chicago, Rosemary Ruether of Howard School of Religion, and Nelle Morton, emerita faculty of Drew Theological Seminary.

In 1972–73 three courses were offered: "Women and Traditional Theological Literature," "New Models of Women in Theology," and "Women: Movement and Tasks." There were also short programs on such topics as new models of partnership in marriage and work, female sexuality and gay/lesbian issues, women and the law, self-help clinics and women's knowledge of their bodies, and women and ministry. 1973–74 saw three courses on female spirituality and women mystics, arranged by Dorothy Donnelly of the Jesuit School of Theology at Berkeley. On January 24 and 25, 1976, the OWA hosted a major two-day conference called "Women, Race and Class" at Pacific Lutheran Theological Seminary. In 1974 Clare Fischer wrote *Woman: A Theological Perspective* and in 1980 *Breaking Through: A Bibliography of Women and Religion*, both published by the GTU.

The center also conducted a survey on women's issues at the GTU in the spring of 1973 and submitted a report on their findings in the fall of 1973 with requests for expanded resources for women, classes on women's issues, and more women faculty. In 1971, when the OWA began, there were only 89 female students and 826 male students at the GTU schools, which had 5 female faculty (only one tenured) and 95 male faculty. In 2005 there were 154 faculty at the GTU schools—101 men and 53 women. Unfortunately, there are still few women of color on the faculty: two Asian women and one African American. Only one woman of color is full-time and tenure track. In 2005, out of 1,328 students, 645 were men, and 682 were women.

Several publications by people associated with the center appeared in the early years. *Women and the Word: Toward a Whole Theology* appeared in 1972, published by the GTU, and *Women in a Strange Land* published by Fortress Press in 1975. Peggy Cleveland's account of the OWA/CWR appeared in the first appendix of *Your Daughters Shall Prophesy: Feminist Alternatives in Theological Education* (Pilgrim Press, 1980).

In the mid-1970s the center was able to secure a sizable Ford Foundation grant, which was used primarily to bring visiting scholars to campus, including Beverly Wildung Harrison and Charlotte Bunch.

Floris Mikkelsen was office coordinator from 1971 to 1973, and Sally Dries from 1973 to 1976. Peggy Cleveland, Madelyn Stelmach, and Barbara Waugh were on the staff from 1977 to 1980. Among the early founders and members of the fifteen-member board of directors were Anne McGrew Bennett, Karen Bloomquist, and Clare Fischer. Barbara Waugh continued as staff until 1983. In 1976–77 the OWA was renamed the Center for Women and Religion. Mary Cross came on as codirector in 1978, and Sandra Park in 1980. In 1981 the newsletter of CWR was expanded into a regular journal, *The Journal of Women and Religion*. Cross and Park remained codirectors from 1983 to 1986. From 1986 to 1989 the codirectors were Mary Cross, Margaret McManus, and Sandra Yarlott. In 1989 Pamela Cooper-White became the first solo director, continuing until 1994. Margaret McManus continued in a consulting role on the staff for several years. Marta Vides was interim director from 1994 to 1996, and Amy Teichman and Sherri Hostetler were interim codirectors from 1996 to 1997. Cheryl Kirk-Duggan was appointed CWR director in February 1997 and continued in that position until the center closed in 2003.

The successive issues of the *Journal of Women and Religion* give some insight into the activities and emphases of CWR in those years. In 1982 members of CWR participated in the Women's Inter-Seminary Conference, and on April 29 and 30 of that year, CWR hosted a major conference of storytelling, liturgy, and workshops, called "Birthing Our Unity." 1984 saw a focus on women's retreats, including the production of a resource publication on women's retreats. In 1986 an annual lecture on women's issues was established in memory of Marjorie Casebier McCoy, a pioneering pastor.

By the late 1980s the work of CWR was organized into three areas: program, curriculum, and publications. An array of programs was offered each year: concerts, dance workshops, and scholarly panels, retreats, and workshops. In 1990 CWR hosted the premiere of *Mother Wove the Morning*, a one-woman play about women in the Bible by Carol Lynn Pearson. The center also participated in the commissioning of an icon of Mary Magdalene for Grace Cathedral in San Francisco.

A quilt honoring women's lives was created as a project of the center as well. Programs and publications in the journal in 1988 focused on women's experience in ordained ministry, on women's faith development in 1989, and on racism and sexism in 1990–91. Religious art was a theme for the journal in 1992, and poor and working-class women and economic justice in 1993. A delegation of GTU women attended the 1995 United Nations Fourth World Conference on Women in Beijing, China, and their experiences at the conference were the focus of that year's issue of the journal. In 1997 the journal published a book-length study by Inna Jane Ray and Cheryl Kirk-Duggan titled "The Atonement Muddle."[2]

The teaching role of the center's director was increased, and full GTU faculty status was granted to Cheryl Kirk-Duggan in 1997. This was a time of prolific feminist writing by women closely associated with CWR, such as Sandra Schneiders, Lynn Rhodes, China Galland, Antoinette ("Ann") Wire, Rosemary Chinnici, Martha Ellen Stortz, Valerie DeMarinis, Pamela Cooper-White, Jane Spahr, Kathryn Poethig, and Melinda McLain. Mary Hunt edited an anthology of the writings of Anne McGrew Bennett.

Cheryl Kirk-Duggan's tenure as director included several major conferences. From February 26 to March 1, 1998, a conference celebrating the history and work of CWR brought together eighteen speakers who also hailed the installation of Cheryl Kirk-Duggan as the new director. The 1999 programs focused on feminist pedagogy, while the 2000 Soul to Soul Conference made "Women, Spirituality, and Health" its theme. The 2001 and 2002 issues of the journal focused on ecofeminism and science and technology. The twentieth volume of the *Journal of Women and Religion*, published in 2002, was the last, and Cheryl Kirk-Duggan announced that the center would close.

REFLECTIONS ON THE EARLY YEARS AT CWR
Peggy H. Cleveland

It has been almost thirty years since I had the privilege of being one of the codirectors of what was then the Office of Women's Affairs at the GTU. Some of my memory may be fogged by time and some of my analysis blurred by subjectivity. Here briefly is an account of what I believe we did—and didn't do—during the two years (1976–78) I was codirector.

Power, in one form or another, was the overarching issue with which we had to contend as we sought a new way to live in the Graduate Theological Union. The work to establish the Office of Women's Affairs had already been done before I joined the staff, so I cannot reflect on that process. The board of the Office of Women's Affairs had decided to have a three-director staff in order to demonstrate our commitment to a model of shared power. A large student work cadre also was an integral part of the staff, another statement of shared power.

Shared power was not a model of leadership in any seminary of the Graduate Theological Union. Our adoption of this model was seen as an anomaly and sometimes as a threat. Our right to make our own decisions on important matters, rather than petitioning for permission from the GTU, was not assured. I cannot forget the scolding we got from our brothers when we decided to change our name from the Office of Women's Affairs to the Center for Women and Religion without asking their permission!

Funding for the Center for Women and Religion was also a major power issue. Although we had to become a sponsored center of the GTU in order to exist, we nevertheless had to make yearly requests for grants to run our programs. These came in varying amounts from the different seminaries, some of which did not provide any funds at all. Thus funding for CWR was marginal. When funding is marginal, the program tends to be viewed by the powers that be as marginal. One can ask whether it was marginal because it was underfunded or whether it was underfunded in order to be kept marginal.

One example of our funding difficulties was in relation to a grant. We applied for and received a grant for $75,000 from the Ford Foundation. The GTU insisted on keeping 23 percent of this grant for administrative purposes, which seemed to us excessive. This left us with $57,000, which we used to bring feminist scholars to campus as part of our effort to challenge and enhance the offerings of the curriculum. The grant money was restricted and could not be used for CWR's own administration. So we had to find those funds elsewhere.

The most serious issue we faced was that of being heard, of finding a voice to articulate the strength and importance we knew were hidden in our stories. Each of our stories was unique, yet each one strengthened the bonds that we were discovering with one another as a sisterhood. In our context we particularly had to find the grace to live and work together as straight women and lesbians. This was an internal staff struggle, as well as a struggle within the larger women's community.

Out of our efforts to survive and strive in theological education and the Christian church, which for millennia had been a bastion of male dominance, we came to realize that the very methods by which theological studies had been taught had to be challenged. We needed to explore not only a new content of theological studies that would include women but also a new pedagogy—how theology is taught. Feminist pedagogy in theological education became a central theme of our work at CWR.

We did a tremendous amount of work. Yet we also made a difference simply by being there. Women in seminary no longer had to wonder, as I did when I was the only woman in my seminary, whether we had landed on another planet. Yet there were also weaknesses in our vision and program for change. Much of this reflected the early stage of our efforts to address a multiplicity of issues at once, none of which had been addressed before.

The interrelation of racism, sexism, and classism was one issue that cried out for incisive analysis, but we were not capable of addressing it adequately at that time. One obvious problem was the lack of students or faculty who were women of color. One can hardly flesh out such an important issue in the abstract, without the living experience of women of color to instruct us and challenge our limitations. There were many more opportunities for antiracism work in the fieldwork assignments for the women active in CWR, and this helped us to address racism. But what antiracism work should mean within theological education was not effectively addressed.

We also failed to make use of what should have been a primary resource for theological students, namely the Bible. The rich cross-fertilization of our work at CWR with women in biblical studies did not take place. I do not remember a single time in which the insights women were learning in their First and Second Testament studies were brought to bear on any issue with which we had to struggle at CWR. Pioneering work was being done by women in the biblical studies field, but even today it has not been brought into dialogue with feminism in other fields.

I think our model of leadership was not fully effective. A major mantra of the women's movement at that time was "The personal is political." But it was not easy when one started with the personal to connect it effectively to the political. We started each meeting with a process of "checking in"; that was our way of addressing the connection of the personal and the political. But when there are three codirectors and eight work-study staff in a two-hour meeting, the personal tended to get in the way of the political. We tended to have a lot more process than product. As a woman trained in an earlier time to prize effective action, I found this to be troubling.

Finally, I have to ask, did we do any good? When I think of the rich, energetic, dedicated, and delightful women who made up the community that was the Center for Women and Religion, I have to conclude that we did an enormous amount of good. Almost thirty-five years of students attending the GTU benefited from this rich community. Even more, those who worked as staff and teachers from the CWR went on to make rich contributions throughout the country and internationally. This network of women who flowed forth from the CWR community is indeed a testimony to its productivity.

"By their fruits you shall know them." Here is a brief list of some of the women who got their feminist beginnings in those first years of CWR and have gone on to make important contributions.

Mary Hunt, early staffer at CWR, with Diane Neu founded the Women's Alliance for Theology, Ethics and Ritual in Silver Spring, Maryland. They have kept it running for more than twenty years. Mary wrote the book *Fierce Tenderness* (1991), coedited *Good Sex* (2001), and edited *A Guide for Women and Religion* (2004).[3] She has helped keep the vision of an inclusive church and ministry alive among her Catholic sisters.

Ann-Cathrin Jarl, a Frontier intern from Sweden, has been ordained in the Church of Sweden. She has served on the staff of the bishop of Stockholm and finished her PhD, publishing her doctoral thesis as *Justice: Women and Global Economics* (Fortress Press, 2003). Her work has been enormously important internationally in making the connections among women, class, and economics.

Loey Powell, an ordained minister in the United Church of Christ, has served both as an associate pastor and as a senior pastor. She is now on the national staff of the United Church of Christ in Cleveland, serving as team leader for the Human Rights, Justice for Women, and Transformation Ministry teams in Justice and Witness Ministries.

Karen Bloomquist chaired the sexuality study for the Evangelical Lutheran Church in America. She is now on the staff of the Lutheran World Federation in Geneva, Switzerland.

Robin Jurs worked hard and faithfully on the Nestle boycott campaign when she was a student. She has since been a staff member at the child care center at Smith College and now directs her own child care program.

When Kim Klein asked what was the most important thing she could do for women, she was told to teach them how to raise money. She went out that day and apprenticed herself to the development officer at the Pacific School of Religion, and then she went on to the task of fund-raising for the campaign about DES (a drug for morning sickness that was being promoted by a coalition for women's health). After she completed that task, she joined the development staff at the Appalachian

Fund and was then called to New York to help the Exchange Fund raise $11 million. Since completing that work, she has become one of the best known and respected fund-raising trainers in the United States. She has published a book that is widely used by nonprofits, *Fundraising for Social Change*. She and her partner, Stephanie, publish the *Grassroots Fundraising Journal*.

After leaving CWR to complete a doctorate at the Wright Institute, Barbara Waugh joined Hewlett-Packard. She used her successive positions as company recruiting manager, personnel director, and worldwide change manager for HP labs to transform Hewlett-Packard's corporate culture. She has told her story in the widely read book *The Soul in the Computer: The Story of a Corporate Revolutionary*.[4]

Stacy Cusolus founded MUSASA, a consulting and training firm. (*Musasa* is an African tree that provides shelter.) She managed training for Tandem in Silicon Valley for three years and for Hewlett-Packard for eight years and is also the author of training curricula.

After her time at CWR, Madelyn Stelmach obtained training in physical therapy at Stanford, a profession she still pursues.

In addition to these women's rich contributions, many others were part of CWR's work in reconfiguring theology and have become major leaders in feminist biblical and theological studies. Among those who worked with CWR in those early years and have since had long careers as teachers, scholars, and writers at the GTU are Ann Wire, Karen Lebacqz, Sandra Schneiders, and Mary Ann Donovan.

Those who were brought to campus under the Ford Foundation grant include Beverly Wildung Harrison, who gave us all the answers many of us were searching for in her great book, *Our Right to Choose*. Beverly completed her long career of teaching at Union Theological Seminary in New York City and now lives in a beautiful community near Brevard, North Carolina, where she writes and keeps a house full of pets.

Rosemary Radford Ruether finished her teaching at Howard University School of Religion in 1975. She moved on to teach at Garrett-Evangelical Theological Seminary in Evanston, Illinois, from 1975 to 2002 and then held the Carpenter Chair of Feminist Theology at the

GTU from 2000 to 2005. She is currently a visiting scholar at the School of Religion and Graduate School in Claremont, California.

Clare Fischer finished her PhD at the GTU, gave us a bibliography in feminist studies in religion that was unparalleled in completeness, and had a long career as a professor at Starr King School for the Ministry.

Charlotte Bunch spent a quarter with us helping us to think through feminist pedagogy. She is the executive director of the Center for Women's Global Leadership at Rutgers University, where she is a tenured professor. She also teaches courses in sexuality and gender studies. She was awarded the Presidential Medal of Honor for her successful work to include the abuse of women in the conventions of the United Nations Human Rights Commission.

Anne Bennett and Nelle Morton have preceded us to glory, but not before a warning from Nelle that the *Journey Is Home*,[5] a realization that we are still a work in progress and every issue we faced in those early days of hope and promise is still with us today.

As pebbles tossed into a pond send their ripples out indefinitely, so the influence of CWR in theological education and ministry continues to be felt locally and through the world.

THE EARLY 1990s
WHOSE CWR? WHOSE FEMINISM?

Pamela Cooper-White

The five years I was director of CWR, 1989–1994, were a time of considerable turmoil—both enormous creative energy and internal organizational conflict. As happened around the same time for many feminist organizations birthed out of the consciousness raising of the early 1970s, CWR reached its twentieth anniversary at a crossroads between the radical vision of an independent, nonhierarchical collective that characterized its origins and the hope for greater institutionalization that emerged over time with a certain degree of "mainstreaming" of its visions and values into its larger context—in this case, the GTU and the growing community of alumnae. When I arrived at CWR, it was governed by a board, comprised predominantly of faculty and alumni, many of whom were ordained Protestant clergy, and a student steering committee, comprised mostly of students pursuing master of divinity and master of arts degrees. The staff were also students.

During this time CWR faced an internal crisis. It had existed as an unincorporated but increasingly financially dependent entity within the GTU. The GTU insisted that CWR become either a regular program unit, with formal lines of accountability to the GTU administration, a model which many of the GTU schools supported, or an independently incorporated nonprofit organization—a "501(c)3"—with its own separate governance. There were perils on both sides of this decision, as those inside the CWR organization saw it: to incorporate meant greater freedom, in particular to do advocacy in the wider community around women's concerns, but possibly would jeopardize the already-dwindling financial support of the nine GTU member seminaries. To become a regular program unit meant sacrificing this autonomy while strengthening ties to the GTU, particularly around the scholarly endeavors of CWR, such as curriculum and research. The pragmatic hope was that this would ensure a level of financial support and security for the continuation of CWR. Some long-time CWR leaders feared, on the other hand, that the GTU would eventually absorb CWR, including its financial assets and donor base, suppress political activism, and "mainstream" CWR out of existence.

This debate brought serious differences to light among CWR's board, staff, students, and member/donor base in relation to views on organizational structure and deeper philosophical visions. We discovered a divergence of feminisms that had evolved among us, largely unnamed, over the past two decades. I intend to be circumspect about my own interpretation of this situation (at a distance now of eleven years and three thousand miles!), since there were so many women associated in one way or another with CWR, and each of us would bring a different interpretation to these years. I have identified three independent, though overlapping, paradigms of feminism operative within CWR's multiple constituencies.

Using the language of the women who adhered to each of these perspectives themselves, I call the first "radical" or "progressive" feminism. This vision predominated when the Office of Women's Affairs was first founded. Grounded in Marxist-feminist ideals (whether conscious or absorbed by osmosis through 1960s radical feminism) related to an alternative, nonhierarchical collective and promoting consciousness raising as a tool for awakening feminist movements for justice, this form of feminism existed as a revered tradition into CWR's third decade. Its main proponents were students, student staff, women who had been involved in the earliest days of CWR and were steeped in the ideals of "second-wave" radical feminism from the 1960s, and others who had been involved in public feminist advocacy and community organizing beyond the GTU. The goal of this form of feminism was essentially revolutionary (even if the form it took in our context was mainly via persuasion and education)—the overthrow of existing structures, patterns, and institutions that perpetuated oppression, and the hope of a new, egalitarian social order.

Within CWR this could be seen, for example, in the class format of CWR courses in which students themselves developed the syllabus and took turns facilitating sessions, and in the vestiges of a student steering committee. It could also be seen in the growing interest among many in being involved in political activism beyond the walls of the GTU, and the research, program, and publications that promoted radical—that is, to-the-root—causes. These included analysis of economic injustice and violence against women and a linking of the oppressions of racism, sexism, heterosexism, classism, and economic and sexual violence against women. Theologically, the radical method tended to be guided by a hermeneutics of suspicion and a rejection of patriarchal images of God that reinforced women's subordination. This strand of feminism was most strongly represented among younger students (under age thirty), CWR staff, and some older (often over fifty) GTU women faculty who had been steeped in radical critical analysis in their own formative years as scholars.

The second form of feminism, which grew in strength within CWR's constituents since the 1980s, was what most of its adherents would simply call "feminism." Social analysts might call this "liberal feminism," while its detractors, as I once heard it named pejoratively by one of the radical student feminists, "NOW-style bourgeois feminism." The goal of liberal feminism was not so much the overthrow of existing social structures as the equal access of women to the privilege, decision making, power, and authority enjoyed by men within those structures. If Marxism was the underlying politics of radical feminism, then Enlightenment values of liberty, brotherhood and sisterhood, and equality were the rallying cry of liberal feminism. In the context of CWR, this strand could be seen in advocacy within the GTU for more women faculty, the promotion of existing women faculty to tenured rank (a very real battle in some member seminaries), and the encouragement of women PhD students and faculty to publish feminist scholarship. In the wider sphere of institutional religion, this meant the ordination of women and efforts to break through the "stained-glass ceiling" of assistant and associate pastorates.

Theologically, at least one wing of the liberal feminist method could be seen—as some PhD students were doing at that time—in the appropriation of the thought and method of major nineteenth- and twentieth-century theologians, such as Karl Barth, Reinhold Niebuhr, and Friedrich Schleiermacher, or that of ancient sources such as Augustine and Thomas Aquinas and the Bible itself. In recovering women's voices and leadership in antiquity, these feminists intended to show that women deserved an equal place of power in church and society. This strand of feminism was probably most represented among CWR's board members, some women faculty and administrators, and growing numbers of GTU alumnae, many of whom were ordained clergy invested in changing the church's injustices from within.

Finally, perhaps emerging mostly in the later 1980s, there was a form of feminism that might be termed "essentialist." In the realm of women and religion, this form of feminism grew out of the women's spirituality movement and existed mainly in conversation with and contrast to liberal feminism. If liberal feminists were seeking equality with men, essentialist feminists were celebrating a model of *essential*, even innate, *differences* between women and men. Like liberal feminists, they advocated for an equal valuation of women but critiqued liberal feminists for "trying to be like men." They embraced a matriarchal or sororal ideal of women as nurturing, intuitive, creative, collaborative, and, like the ideal of their radical feminist sisters, nonhierarchical. Their vision, however, was more utopian than revolutionary per se. Often somewhat separatist in their spiritual practices, many of these women sought to recover or reconstruct ancient and premodern forms of goddess worship and "women's ways of knowing," which could be taught and practiced by both women and men alike.

This strand of feminism cast a wide net, including some Jungians, Wiccans, ecofeminists, and the feminist spirituality movement. Some examples of this strand within CWR are China Galland's work as a research fellow of CWR on the Black Madonna,[6] using a methodology of incorporating autobiography, pilgrimage, and intuitive journalism; Carol Lynn Pearson's regional premiere, cosponsored by CWR, of the one-woman play *Woman Wove the Morning*, depicting women's spirituality throughout history from prehistoric to biblical to modern times; and some of the spiritual retreats that were offered by students and guest facilitators from the wider community. Although it was popular as part of many of CWR's programs, this strand was probably the least represented in CWR's innermost circles of board, staff, and current students but was to be found among some CWR members and women in the wider community who sought CWR as a place of hospitality for nurturing women's spirituality.

Notably, there was at the time little participation by—and only beginning attention to—womanist, black feminist, *mujerista*, Asian, and "two-thirds-world" feminist voices, as well as lesbian voices, which were beginning to emerge in both religious institutions and the academy. Many of us began to urge greater diversity in terms of women of color, non-Christian women, and also lesbian and bisexual women on our staff and board and in our publications and programs. We made some important inroads and opened some dialogue—particularly through our courses and our growing relationship with American Baptist Seminary of the West, which had the most racial diversity of the nine GTU member schools at that time; our increase in linkages with Jewish and Buddhist women scholars, rabbis, and monks; and our uneasy, brief interaction with the underground collective Seminary Lesbians Under

Theological Stress ("SLUTS"). But we were still a largely straight white organization, and the forms of feminism represented were for the most part still informed by various brands of white European modernist assumptions.

Postmodern feminism, and post-structuralism in general, were also just beginning to be explored in some classes (for example, in some of the work that was emerging at Starr King School) and in some doctoral students' readings. But at least during the time I was at CWR, few of us were reading, much less engaging in dialogue knowledgeably with, contemporary European expressions of feminist thought, gender theory in cultural studies, queer theory, and works on gender by American postmodern theorists influenced by psychoanalysis, such as Jane Flax and Judith Butler.

One can see how these differences could become sources of conflict at a time when CWR was under pressure to redefine itself organizationally—especially conflict between the radical and the liberal feminists who largely comprised CWR's leadership. Radical feminists were most uncomfortable with becoming an official program unit under the GTU's governance, fearing that patriarchal institutional structures of the GTU and its member schools (who had no female presidents, having lost Barbara Brown Zikmund from the Pacific School of Religion precisely during that time, and few women deans) were becoming more, rather than less, complacent. Like members of any radical feminist organization founded on a collective model, CWR's leaders and members expressed grave concern about any bow to hierarchical organization, including the idea of having employees, including a director with a line of accountability to deans and presidents and ultimately to a governing board of trustees whose *primary* agenda was not feminism or radical social change but overall institutional preservation and growth. Radical feminists saw most clearly the dangers of being co-opted, turning a blind eye to racism, and allowing the crumbs of tokenism to satisfy white feminists' yearnings for inclusion at the table of power without "lifting others as we climb."[7]

As liberal feminists joined the organization in greater numbers, however, the values of bringing feminist issues into the wider curriculum of the schools, supporting and encouraging women clergy and scholars, and ensuring justice for women within institutional structures of church and academia were also recognized and affirmed as important. Women guided by this model saw value in strengthening ties to the GTU and the denominational judicatories of church bodies related to the various seminaries in order to provide an avenue to highlight women's contributions and to raise up women within these structures as well as educate men about the struggle for women's liberation. Liberal feminists tended to see most clearly some of the pitfalls of an unstructured collective—such as the potential for the exercise of covert or charismatic power under the guise of resisting authority and the draw of such an organization for women whose unhealed wounds could generate reflexive, unreflective expressions of anger with little appreciation for the benefits of appropriate uses of authority.

In 1993, after a protracted four-year struggle, including the formation of a futures committee representing CWR's multiple constituencies and a subsequent implementation committee, the CWR board decided to affirm CWR's status as an official program unit of the GTU. Within the same time frame, CWR worked through a painful process of cutbacks in staff and program to achieve a zero-deficit budget.

Not surprisingly, many of the published writings of women closely affiliated with CWR during this period grappled with women's experiences of victimization and oppression and with ethical questions and dynamics of power. These included *Co-creating: A Feminist Vision of Ministry* (1987) by CWR board member Lynn Rhodes of Pacific School of Religion;[8] *From Woman Pain to Woman Vision: Writings in Feminist Theology* (1989), an anthology in honor of one of CWR's founders, Anne McGrew Bennett, edited by Mary Hunt;[9] *The Corinthian Woman Prophets: A Reconstruction through Paul's Rhetoric* (1990) by Ann Wire of San Francisco Theological School;[10] *Can Women Re-image the Church?* (1992) by Rosemary Chinnici of San Francisco School of Theology;[11] *PastorPower* (1993) by Martha Ellen Stortz of Pacific Lutheran Theological School;[12] *Critical Caring: A Feminist Model for Pastoral Psychotherapy* (1994) by Valerie DeMarinis of Pacific School of Religion;[13] *The Cry of Tamar: Violence Against Women and the Church's Response*, my own book (published in 1995);[14] and *Called Out: The Voices and Gifts of Lesbian, Gay, Bisexual and Transgendered Presbyterians* (1995), edited by San Francisco Theological Seminary alumna Jane Spahr, CWR board member Kathryn Poethig, and Melinda McLain.[15]

In an article in the CWR newsletter in 1994, Professor Til Evans of Starr King School for Ministry and I attempted to articulate the more-or-less consensus that finally emerged after much difficulty to undergird the decision to be come a program unit. Three points were highlighted; the first was as follows:

> CWR's identity is inextricably entwined with the GTU. Unlike other organizations which exist to offer resources on feminist spirituality CWR is unique in its grounding in traditional religious institutions. It stands in dialogue with classical theology, and brings its resources, challenges and critiques from within traditional theological educa-tion, and preparation for professional ordained ministry in mainline religions.[16]

CWR's identity was thus affirmed as both interfaith and in continu-ity with mainline Christian theological traditions. The second and third points were stated in this way:

> CWR differs from some of the other centers at the GTU in that its work has never been only academic/research-oriented, or only "stu-dent services," although it embraces both of these. From its found-ing, CWR has owned a primary purpose of advocacy for feminist theology and justice for women. . . . Choosing to affirm our status within the GTU is a decision which affirms our longstanding rela-tionships with each of the GTU schools, and our faith in our ability to carry on constructive, mutual dialogue around issues of justice for women. . . .[17]
>
> CWR's strength does not need to be defined in an over/against or separate/than posture, which to some extent a decision to incorpo-rate might have implied. CWR is the women who exercise leadership within and through its programs, courses and publications. The vast majority of these women are students, faculty, staff and alumnae of GTU schools.[18]
>
> In our conclusion, we stated:

We came to our decision in the end because we believed in the feminist value of staying in relation. We embraced our history within the GTU community, and discerned that our base of power was not apart from that community, but internal to it. In this way, we are a voice not only moving "from margin to center,"[19] but we are also capable because of our proximity of stirring the center with power and passion like a centrifugal force.

It may also be possible to gain some wisdom from this period in CWR's history from a psychodynamic group relations perspective, which some of us were trying to discern at the time but is perhaps even clearer in hindsight. At the time, some of us came to see CWR as going through a kind of organizational adolescence. No longer in its formative infant years, the organization as a whole was seeking a mature identity and structure. While I would now question the linearity of a developmental progress model as applied to that period, there are some elements in the metaphor of adolescence that describe the passage of transition we were undergoing. In our desire to clarify our relations with the GTU, we were torn between our desires for nurture and security by a larger entity and our needs for autonomy and self-determination. Like many adolescents, CWR struggled with both identity formation and identity diffusion.[20] Diffusion was perhaps represented by the proliferation of feminist models under one roof.

The search for identity was seen as we fought vehemently among ourselves about what priorities would dictate the use of our time and the talents we wanted to encourage and cultivate among our students, staff, and membership. There was ambivalence about the ordination of women—and this was regarded quite differently by feminists of different stripes. More generally, we all longed in one way or another for authority that we could both rely upon and take turns in exercising ethically, yet we also feared authority—because we had internalized our own oppression and experienced it wielded against us in its most violent patriarchal forms. My decision to reenter ordained ministry during my time as director may have further stirred anxieties and questions about women's authority and appropriate relationship to institutional structures. As an organization we enacted a love-hate relationship with the quasi-parental figures of seminary deans and presidents and, at times, within CWR also, as (often younger) staff and students came into conflict with (often older) board members.

A recognition of these dynamics is reflected in the article by Til Evans and myself in these terms:

> CWR, we believe, achieved a new stage of psychological maturity in reaching the recognition that an accountability-*free* relationship was impossible. . . . The decision was then reframed from avoidance of accountability to asking what relationship would involve the greatest *mutuality*? . . . Unlike much of patriarchally conditioned psychology, this ["mature dependence," in which mutuality and reciprocity are valued,] is a view which conforms better to women's experience and culture, as also described in Jean Baker Miller's *New Psychology of Women*,[21] and the Stone Center's model of psychological health and maturity defined not as individualism but as "self-in-relation. . . ."[22] CWR is now positioned to move, to act, and to speak from a knowledge and sense of ourselves as a religiously feminist organization, and to have impact on the larger organization and community of which we are a part. . . . We are inviting, demanding, claiming dialogue. . . . The greatest risk ahead of us is losing courage. Yes, this means entering into "ambiguity and risk." . . . We are in a time of newness and transition. We must feel our way. How will we live out this newly affirmed relatedness as concrete challenges face us?[23]

At a deeper, unconscious level, I also believe that my pregnancy, and perhaps the subsequent pregnancies of two younger women (one staff, one student), also increased the unconscious anxiety in the CWR "system," just as it was coming to terms with these growing pains. Challenges to organizational structure in particular are often felt unconsciously in groups as a threat to the body of the mother.[24] The externalization of unconscious fantasies about parenting and being parented in the form of a very pregnant director; feelings of both abandonment and freedom from oversight during my maternity leave; and adjustments both organizational and emotional that ensued upon my return—with infant—triggered unconscious struggles around competition for care and attention, but also eventually a new level of maturity as the realities of women's lives became incorporated into the life of the organization.

In the language of British psychoanalyst Melanie Klein, the danger of an organization struggling with such complex issues involving potential changes in both structure and missional focus is the danger of splitting, or falling into what she termed a "paranoid-schizoid position"[25] of relating to the world within and around us. Such splitting engenders an organizational climate in which the group's conscious task may become submerged under unconscious tendencies toward dependency, fight/flight, or the formation of isolated pair-bonds within the larger group.[26] When we were at our worst, competing and excluding one another over who was a "true feminist," or operating out of our fears more than our common hopes and potentials, I believe we did fall into this mode of being. The hurts we inflicted on one another when in this mode were profound. And yet many voices throughout this time, from a variety of philosophical backgrounds, were calling for holding the center, working to extricate ourselves from our own temptations toward splitting, and trying to listen fairly to a multiplicity of perspectives.

Maturity, in Kleinian terms, requires a capacity for holding good and bad together in the same perception of reality, neither claiming the innocent high ground for oneself nor projecting all the causes of evil and harm outside onto others—particularly authority figures who stimulate unconscious memories of infantile aggression and dependency. At our best, I believe that we managed, at least some of the time, to grieve the utopias that we could not achieve but also to embrace a complex hope for greater collaboration, to claim and exercise a mature power within realistic limits, and to work toward a wider diversity both within CWR and in our collaboration with other GTU entities and beyond the GTU.

Our Contributions

As hard as it may be to believe, given the intensity of these years, many of these struggles were probably invisible to the wider circle affiliated with CWR. I remember at the time that board members often commented on CWR's amazing productivity and the continued creativity of its staff, in spite of the turmoil we often felt internally.

CWR's several hundred members were nourished in their far-flung contexts largely through the CWR newsletter and *Journal of Women and Religion*. The wider student population of the GTU schools was consistently nourished and inspired by CWR's prodigious output in both program and curriculum. Each year an exciting array of both public programs and courses for credit was offered, representing a variety of feminist perspectives. Concerts, dance workshops, scholarly panels, spiritual retreats, support groups, and workshops were offered on a regular basis every September through June, drawing leadership from both within and outside the GTU faculty and student body. The annual *Journal of Women and Religion,* which was broadly subscribed to by theological libraries nationally and even internationally, was an annual published symposium of scholarly reflections on subjects including women's faith development, racism and sexism, religious art, and poor- and working-class women and economic justice.

Conclusion: Looking to the Future

In 1994 I was called away to Chicago to a new chapter of my life. How the fears or hopes of existing or emerging feminisms—radical, liberal, essentialist, or multicultural—would flourish at CWR (before it went into hiatus in 2003) would be up to Cheryl Kirk-Duggan, who became director in 1997. But whatever forms feminism (plural) is taking and will take at the GTU from today forward, CWR has left a lasting legacy of profound and challenging thought and advocacy for future generations—not only seeds, to quote Mary Hunt, but also flowers that bloomed in their own season. It is my hope that in moving forward, a wide array of radical, pragmatic, woman-affirming, and increasingly diverse women's spiritual, religious, ethical, and theological thought—premodern, modern, and postmodern—will be given a forum for both reflection and action, with particular attention to the increasing racial, ethnic, sexual, cultural, and religious diversity of women's voices.

My primary concern, after attending the day-long symposium celebrating CWR's history and envisioning a future for women's studies

at the GTU, is that as feminist theologians and feminists deeply concerned with religion, we are still mostly talking—refining, redefining,
arguing, and nuancing differences—among ourselves. The median age
of the audience at this conference seemed much older than at typical
CWR events in the early 1990s. While a women's studies concentration
would be a strong addition to the GTU's options for committed feminist
scholars, it is my conviction that more is needed. My vision is that every
seminary require *every* student, both male and female—and dare I say,
every faculty member!—to study and become conversant with the now
three decades of profound contributions made by feminist, womanist,
mujerista, Asian, and global women theologians.

In addition, we should be willing to seek out greater opportunities to put forth our own feminist writings, and the insights of feminist
theological thought more generally, in nonfeminist settings (whether
classrooms, conferences, journals, or other publishing venues) for the
purpose of mutual dialogue and critique with others who are not imme-
diately convinced of its significance. This could help sharpen our own
arguments and would put our own assumptions to the test of broader
scholarly inquiry. We know from experience that we cannot guarantee
the universal *acceptance* of feminist work, but its *recognition* as important—both as radical critical method and as creative theological construct—is something for which we should continue to advocate with
passion and determination. Feminist theology in all its forms and multi-
religious perspectives as well as serious, culturally diverse studies of
women's issues in religion deserve to be vigorously argued and confi-
dently defended in wider academic and religious arenas. Only when this
body of work by feminist theologians is considered part of the canon, to
be digested and contended with by all educated students and teachers
of theology, can the full import of feminist theologies make a real difference—in this time of emboldened conservatism in both church and
society, when it is all the more needed.

DREAMS, VISIONS, AND DISCONNECTS
Cheryl A. Kirk-Duggan

In Memoriam: The Rev. Mary Ellen Gaylord

Having heard the voice of Spirit, of God,
Speak to her and say:
"Come on, Daughter, go forth and proclaim,"
She shuddered, realizing, knowing
The chaos that comes with people's faith
And that she, in Aristotelian terms,
Was not seen as one of suitable gender
Since she is really an incomplete man;
She chuckled to herself and said:
"Surely, God, you jest."
Why would you call me to do ministry,
To preach and teach,
When lots of men on faculty, in administrations,
In churches, dioceses, conventions, and associations
Will not respect me?
They have this Abrahamic ilk
About me being from a spare part of some man;
Connected to the notion that it's women's fault
That some adamah didn't have enough sense
To not eat some mythical fruit
And allegedly be the root cause, the origins,
Of the problems we have today.
How horribly misconstrued they are.

And why should I
Subject myself, the wonderful self you created,
To a life of misery and hostility,
Sometimes not so much for those of the male persuasion
But also some of those females who are
So bent over, so oppressed, so paranoid, so jealous, so fearful
That they will give me as much grief as the men.
So what's the point?
And God / Spirit said:
"You give me all of these excuses,
Yet I created you wonderfully, marvelously.
Think not that genitalia makes for magnificence;

It is not the component for measuring excellence.
Listen to the voice within, and know who you are;
Know where you are to create
A brand-new world, building upon legacies of your
Sisters and brothers who have gone before you.
This is not a man's world, though many think it is;
This is still my world, human beings are stewards
Given the gift of life, to live in community."
And so she said,
Let me stand tall and strong;
Let me go and meet my sisters
And tell them what you have told me:
That we are made wonderfully;
We are to meet and create and take charge.

And so she said,
And so they did,
and they met and created
A grassroots organization
Tucked in upon Holy Hill.
Instigating from the inside,
Making a difference often on the outside.
Yet alas, the whole community
Never got the vision.
And so they worked and worked and worked
And, despite odds, excelled in excellence
And changed lives
And made international connections
And groomed leaders
And honored many
And fought magnificent causes
And then—was no more.

The reality of patriarchy, racism, hegemony, and sexism alongside of institutional, communal, and individual fear, manipulation, and a perceived need to control makes it clear that women in general, and women in religion in particular, have not yet arrived in the groves of secular and religious academe. While numerous seminaries and theological unions boast of their student bodies with 50 percent or more women, rarely can those same seminaries boast of 25 percent, let alone 50 percent, tenured women faculty. One can graduate from many so-called liberal seminaries and take male-directed classes in which not only does the subject matter not include women but the required reading list is devoid of female authors.

While the numbers of women students may be significant, the capacity of women to have nonadministrative power in the seminary and to be considered as the first choice for pastorships after seminary based upon their master of divinity or doctorate in ministry is often nil to marginal at best. Many times women with Ph.D.s in religion and religious studies have to scrape and hustle above and beyond their male peers to get hired in tenure-track positions. These facts notwithstanding, that then President Lawrence Summers of Harvard could make the statements he made about women's alleged innate genetic inferiority (in terms of succeeding in science and engineering) lets us know that in many respects, women have not "come a long way, baby"—not at all.

This sociocultural reality of women's historical exclusion was one of the reasons that female students and a very few male and female faculty first launched the Office of Women's Affairs in 1970. They needed a safe place where women could think, relate, and strategize *together*. Religious studies, with a focus on women's issues, was a latecomer to the feminist movement. CWR was birthed and became a reality only eight years after the birth of the Graduate Theological Union itself.

In its most recent iteration, CWR's mission stated that the center's calling was to "promote diverse women's voices in cutting-edge theological education for spiritual growth and social change." CWR was "to be recognized as a significant site for both the study of women in religion and a supportive place to develop women's religious leadership." Such were the lofty and necessary goals for the empowerment of women to serve in the ministries of the academy and faith communities in the twenty-first century. CWR was the oldest such organization for women's issues focusing on religion, spirituality, and theology. An interfaith and multicultural center, CWR was both an academic program unit of the Graduate Theological Union and a nonprofit organization seeking to transform religious and societal injustice and to help women overcome oppression in faith communities and the larger society. The CWR provided academic and community-based programs, sponsored social justice causes, participated internationally in the study and discussion of women and religion, and published a quarterly newsletter and annual journal. So what went wrong? Why was the CWR closed?

Disdainful Indifference

Though there is much beauty and possibility in the world, I sense a brooding instability—what I would call a *disdainful indifference*,[27] which operates as a mitigating factor to the practice and significance of religion in people's lives. What is this disdainful indifference?

It is an attitude and way of thinking that depreciates and devalues the vitality of religious practice and manifests itself in numerous ways. Such disinterest is devoid of analytical, critical, and systematic thinking about the consistency or cruelty in particular statements of faith and tends to live in denial about systemic, institutional violence and the diminishing of individual gifts. This pathology assumes privilege, is often elitist, and takes a certain kind of proprietary glee in establishing disdainful indifference as the elect or the chosen group. Disdainful indifference embodies a style of cheap grace, a naïveté, and a need to control, wherein charisma or credentials mask mediocrity and incompetence. Institutional silence is the order of the day when it comes to exposing leadership incompetence; shallow, irrelevant faith practices; and ineffectiveness in making a difference within the lives of believers or the world beyond. Disdainful indifference emerges in the internal spheres of training and praxis and in the external realm of disinterested belief.

Within seminaries, schools of theology, and departments of religion, the squabbles often become intensely petty, and an awareness of the potential impact of these internecine battles on graduate students is often missing. One notes the truism that the battles of academe are so vicious because the stakes are so trivial, attributed to Henry Kissinger. Like most educational institutions, those that teach religion have standards to meet; boards, dioceses, or conventions to satisfy; and students to please. Because the institutional fights within the seminaries, theological schools, and departments of religion are ferocious, *especially* because the stakes are truly insignificant, pettiness and personality clashes often skew the theological impact of the religious training. (One is reminded that all twelve-step recovery programs emphasize placing principles before or instead of personalities.) Many professors of religion are not trained to teach, and they resist any instruction in pedagogical methods as irrelevant to their areas of perceived expertise. And of course, some who teach religion possess no personal or particular faith commitment, except to a civil religion based upon secular mores.

The battle continues as to whether, in a secular-oriented institution, there should be a named department of religion or religious studies or a school of divinity, subsumed under a liberal arts and sciences umbrella. This internecine warfare over the label on an area of scholarly concentration ignores and obscures the substance of what is being taught or should be taught in such departments. One notes that what is presently subsumed under the name "science" was formerly labeled "natural philosophy." The fight over the name of the department that includes religion within its mission usually ignores the vacuity of the course instructions. Some faculty, particularly those in administrative decision-making positions, grow incredibly nervous when a professor claims passionate faith because they fear proselytizing rather than appreciate personal aesthetic faith.

Passionate agnosticism does not meet with the same administrative scrutiny, skepticism, and fear of exposure. In fact, agnosticism and atheism are often considered both necessary and sufficient hallmarks of tenured professors of philosophy within and outside of seminaries! This is not to say that one cannot have a subdued spiritual life and be a successful teacher within the religious arena. Much of the infighting, the exhaustive committee work, and the confusion on how to realize the mission statement, however, leads to both intolerance and intellectual arrogance springing from a perceived nondenominational relativistic superiority. The incompetence in creating an environment in which knowledge can be experienced on a subject that is very personal for some merely exacerbates the irrelevance and insensitivity in the way religion is taught in the secular and nondenominational classroom. Internally, that disdainful indifference ethos often trickles over to practitioners of organized religion.

Worldwide, there is a diminishing interest in institutionalized and dogmatic faith practices. Many cathedrals, particularly in Europe, have become libraries, museums, or governmental office buildings. Globally, many large sanctuaries are totally empty during the worship hour, while they are thronged during foreign tourist tours. Many local inhabitants find no value in standardized religious services, particularly given the accompanying political infighting and exclusiveness. Some religious paradigms and faith practices make no sense to twenty-first-century people. Others have been shunned, scandalized, or abused by religious clergy, and when the laity protested, the messengers were scapegoated and the message denied. Most religions have never acknowledged—let alone atoned for—their complicity in historical and current world violence. Rather than be subjugated by antiquated doctrine, mediocrity, or messianic complexes, many citizens have now opted for the civil religion of national league sports, gardening, travel, and the observance of Sabbath as a day of rest, relaxation, or frenetic recreation.

Others experience *disdainful indifference* because they see no hope or true community within faith-based institutions, so they would rather put their time and money elsewhere. With increases in violence, the cost of living, and the stress of modern life, many have become jaded and not only question the value of organized religion but, like the protagonist in the *Brothers Karamazov*, ask: "Where is God?" and "If God exists, why do all these evil things happen to innocent people?" (The modern expression in a popular self-help *New York Times* best seller is *When Bad Things Happen to Good People*.[28] The loss of 200 million lives in the twentieth century as a result of government-sponsored violence (combat, biological warfare, economic sanctions) is an indictment against the relevance of religion. Heightened fundamentalist tendencies in religious beliefs, which are reflected in governmental practices (welfare reform, reversal of affirmative action, etc.), test the vitality and boundaries of religion. Theories and theologies without praxis and credible ethics will only perpetuate apathy and ambivalence, which will erode a way of being that has energized human life, culture, and meaningfulness. All persons in leadership, then, and particularly women, have an uphill fortress to climb given the current pathos. How did society and various academic institutions amid disdainful indifference help thwart CWR?

Societal and
Institutional Challenges:
Historic Accomplishments

My reflections may cause some to feel uncomfortable. While this occasion, much like an Irish wake, is a celebration with remembrance, we must speak truth to power. Here I name (not blame) the reality so that whatever program goes forth from this event can learn from the wonderful accomplishments of CWR, at the same time learning from CWR's and GTU's mistakes.

In one sense, CWR was doomed to fail from its inception, because it began as a grassroots effort that later was folded into the GTU in a somewhat ad hoc fashion. Grassroots efforts can only be nominally successful, unless there are sufficient numbers of interested parties with means who are willing to support the project without usurping or co-opting the fledgling organization. An outsider can instigate and make noise, pointing out the flaws and ways in which the status quo is found lacking. Once an outsider becomes part of the establishment, it becomes increasingly difficult to point out the various institutional foibles, particularly acts of oppression and insensitivity to the challenges that exist. Though the agreement was for CWR to be a program unit and thus supported by the GTU, it was regarded as an affiliate, an organization that worked in tandem with the GTU but was required to be self-supporting with non-GTU sources of funding. Had CWR been a directive of the GTU board of trustees, the problems leading to the demise of CWR would not have arisen.

CWR became part of the institution, yet the institution never fully embraced CWR. The Graduate Theological Union never had the funding to support CWR fully when it became something of a tenth school within the GTU. The nine member schools never fully supported CWR, although some schools did a better job than others. For example, some schools funded CWR at the same level in 1998 as they did in 1988, despite inflationary pressures. Some reduced their dollar support for CWR. Thus CWR's directors were put in the precarious position of having to raise their own salaries and funds for any projects the center undertook. The directors had to manage mostly volunteer staff until the last seven years, and they created all of the programming. Funding from the schools partially paid for staff and minimal programming. Recent directors, for all intents and purposes, had to do four jobs. They had to make bricks without straw and with a tiny bit of mud. The member schools gave lip service to support, but many of them did not put their financial or faculty support where their mouths were. Recently, troubles have been threefold: the changing needs of women, the understanding of those needs, and the inability of faculty and administrators to step up to the plate and support CWR.

When CWR first began, there was a need for a safe space to convene, the creation of resources and rituals, and a place that could physically be identified as a place for women. While women populate all of our campuses today, let us not forget that thirty years ago, this was not the case. With the ending of the twentieth century, in some places women did not need this same kind of support. And because by that time member schools could readily count the numbers of female students, they did not really understand why women still needed a center. Yes, the numbers of women students have increased to the point at which women outnumber men in some seminaries within the GTU, and this is to be celebrated. Problematically, while the numbers of female students have increased, sexism and the thwarting of women's empowerment have not gone out of existence. Most of the member schools continue to have substantially more male than female faculty. Some of the member schools have only two or three full-time female faculty. Some have only one. *In 2005 only one of the nine member schools had a tenured female faculty of color.* In 2005 there was *no* full-time Chicana/Latina/Hispanic female faculty at any of the member schools. One Asian woman was on tenure track. Thus female presence in the student body is not matched by the numbers of female faculty.

Second, there are numerous classes taught at the GTU that do not include the voices of women in subject matter or in required readings. This should not be the case in the twenty-first century, and it begs the question about the existence of courses pertaining to or including the voices of Native Americans, Latinos/Latinas/Hispanics/Chicanas,[29] Asian Americans, and African Americans, especially in a multicultural state like California. Third, the fact that student numbers are not indicative of power, access, or importance has been made clear time and time again in history, most recently in the case of South Africa. Fourth, what will female students who graduate with a master of divinity or doctorate in ministry and are affiliated with churches that do not yet ordain women do with their degrees? Would these women find employment easier with social work credentials instead of faith-based degrees? What about those graduating with a Master of Arts? Do the member schools and the GTU have a moral obligation to make sure that graduates are equipped so that they can go out and do a variety of ministries and use their degrees?

The pathology of oppression has thwarted the health and flourishing of CWR several times over. A lack of financial support and system-wide critical thinking and planning during the transition instituted in 2000 meant that CWR's strategic goals would not be met. A lack of system-wide strategizing also means that many of our graduates will end up being bitter about their experiences because they went into debt to come here, to live here, and to receive a sheepskin that does not help them make a living wage.

Along with systemic problems is the particular challenge that arises when women work with each other. When oppression is alive and well, and when those who have been oppressed gain access to power, often they either oppress or lose the ability to support those who are still down and out. Such is the case with some faculty women in recent years. During the latter 1990s and early 2000s, two to three GTU female faculty members served on CWR's board. They contributed their time and their resources, notably in the persons of Karen Lebacqz and Sharon Thornton. Others often wanted to be supportive but had too many commitments, had become disenchanted, or had been persuaded by a variety of sources that supporting CWR was not worth their time and would hinder their professional careers. When faculty women were no longer present on the CWR board and could not help in supporting its cause at their member institutions, then those member schools also no longer saw CWR as a priority.

After the dot-com bust and in the midst of a weakening economy, some member schools began to withdraw some of their support from CWR. In at least one instance, the member school's administration failed to alert CWR that it was withdrawing all of its support. CWR staff learned this secondhand from the dean of the GTU. For some of the member schools, CWR became an albatross and a money pit rather than a place where viable programming could occur for their students, faculty, and staff. Some wanted something more and different from CWR but would not enable the center to raise the funds to extend its programming.

When CWR, along with some women faculty—most recently Ann Wire, Randi Walker, Rosemary Chinnici, Clare Fischer, Rosemary Ruether, and Rebecca Parker—were able to call the faculty women together, we could hear the fatigue in their voices from overcommitment. Scheduling became more and more difficult, and the once- or twice-a-semester gatherings decreased in frequency to about once a year. With faculty facing the demands of their member schools, the doctoral program of the GTU, and their personal lives, it was more difficult to have a representative number gathered. When some faculty women left the GTU to teach in other places, their member schools did not recruit a woman to fill the open position.

Having spoken about some of the challenges, what can we say is the legacy of CWR? First, it is rich and vast. Over the years hundreds of women have come through CWR's programs, classes, conferences, and other events and found their voices. The classes CWR offered launched experimental courses in interdisciplinary studies, including myriad topics from the arts, literature, music, and ecology to film, ritual, ministry, and pedagogy. Several doctoral students gained a great deal of experience in pedagogy and epistemology through designing and teaching CWR courses.

Second, CWR and the GTU have been privileged to host four international conferences in recent years. The February 1998 conference, Soul to Soul: Women, Religion, and the Twenty-first Century, served as my installation as the first full-time paid director and as a grand opportunity to bring an interfaith community together to honor women, with then First Lady Hillary Rodham Clinton as honorary chairperson. The four-day conference featured panels of scholars from across the country. For the opening installation event, the service began with an electrifying call to prayer by an imam; Elisabeth Schüssler Fiorenza was the keynote speaker. The conference culminated with an interfaith service in which the Rt. Rev. Leontine Kelly, retired bishop of the United Methodist Church, brought people to their feet. For both public worship events, a stellar interfaith choir sang music ranging from anthems to gospel and spirituals. Some of the attendees came from as far away as Japan and Germany. CWR also cosponsored the Women and Religion International Symposium with the Tenri Yamato Culture Congress in Tenri, Japan, in July 1998.

The 2000 conference honoring CWR's thirtieth anniversary, Soul to Soul II: Women, Spirituality, and Health, was a collaborative conference, cosponsored by CWR, the Center for Theology and the Natural Sciences, the Pacific School of Religion, Mills College, and the Institute for Research on Women and Gender (IRWG) at Stanford University. This was a riveting and life-changing event for many. Presenters included internationally renowned scholars, activists, and consultants: Jean Kilbourne, noted for her work on women's body images and research on how alcohol and tobacco affect the body; bell hooks, noted scholar and writer; Jean Shinoda Bolen, MD, physician, healer, Buddhist practitioner; Anita de Frantz, head of the Amateur Athletic Foundation, Los Angeles, and an International Olympic Committee member; and panelists on issues related to food: Kilbourne, Laura Fraser, Michelle Lelwica, and Marya Hornbacher. Composer Peter Bellinger set some of the work of Jewish feminist Marcia Falk to music, which premiered at the conference. The Carla de Sola dance troupe also performed.

In addition, were numerous concurrent sessions (interactive, theoretical, and practical). The Rev. Della Reese served as honorary chairperson. One participant who was clearly in spiritual, emotional, and physical distress told conference organizers, "This conference changed my life!" In the realm of liberatory and empowerment praxis and pedagogy, it does not get much better than that.

The final CWR-sponsored conference was Soul 2 Soul III: Women and Science, Technology, and Religion, held in 2001. This local and more strictly academic conference was also well received.

Throughout the ups and downs of my tenure as director, one person who significantly embodied much of what CWR set out to accomplish was Rev. Mary Ellen Gaylord, who died in 2001. She was a GTU trustee and friend of CWR. She had affiliated with CWR since the late 1970s, when she began her participation as an MDiv student at the Pacific School of Religion. Mary Ellen joined CWR's ranks and became an active participant and a staunch supporter. After graduating with her master's degree in 1981, she was ordained in the United Church of Christ in 1983. Her ministerial focus was women's issues and women's needs, particularly how to support women pastors, many of whom were cut off from the support of a community of women. Her interest in the GTU originated with her involvement with CWR. She observed the resources CWR provided for women to come together, particularly in the 1970s, when there were few women in ministry. She always envisioned that CWR would be able to continue its support to the community. In recognition of the center's twenty-fifth anniversary, because of her commitment to women's issues and women's needs, and out of love for the center, she established the CWR scholarship.

Mary Ellen's motivation in establishing the scholarship was the significant need for student financial aid that the GTU experiences. At one time she served as the liaison for all of the centers and affiliates of the GTU. Her passion for strengthening and transforming women's religious experiences pervaded all the causes she supported. Mary Ellen was also instrumental in ensuring that the CWR contingent attended the United Nations Fourth World Conference on Women in Beijing, China, in 1995, and she worked hard to secure long-term support for CWR's operational funds. (Although she bequeathed a half million dollars to the center, as a result of the dot-com bust and after settling all of the family's business matters, CWR did not receive any monies.)

Mary Ellen was a woman of greatness before coming to the GTU and since. The mother of ten children, she had a bounty of love and care. She loved sailing and was a marvelous advocate for justice. A preacher, she served with compassion and faithfulness. She was a spitfire who brought much joy and kindness wherever she went! If she were here, she would say, "The plans we made have not been in vain but have not reaped the harvest that we had intended, so how can we regroup and move on?" In her spirit, I reflect on a dream for empowering women in the twenty-first century.

A Twenty-First-Century Empowering Space for Women

I have had so many hopes and dreams for CWR. Under my leadership the center reached new heights in staffing, programming, and professionalization of our periodicals. We completed the publication of volume 20 of the *Journal of Women and Religion*, and people in the Bay Area and the world came to know about CWR and the GTU. After seven years, it was time for me to take flight and soar in other arenas.

Like Mary McCleod Bethune, who in her will wrote, "I leave you love, I leave you hope and I leave you faith,"[30] I leave you loving passion, a passion for justice to grow a program in a space that honors the gifts and graces of all women; that pushes women to heights of excellence; that teaches them to love themselves well; that builds interdisciplinary curricula; that is intentional in bringing women together across lines of race, faith, class, age, sexual orientation, and political persuasion and in helping men learn to live and work with women. I leave you hope, that you might dream big, know healing, and never give up; that you might work within patriarchal and hegemonic systems to turn them upside down; that your hope will be elastic enough to let you be down when things go wrong but not out; that your hope will fuel the passions of those women who have become jaded and given up, those who are too tired to care anymore; that you have the hope to inspire those women and men who have the creative energies, the financial resources, and the political clout to shape a program of women's studies steeped in theory, in historical lived experience, toward a praxis of accountability and sustainability on Holy Hill.

I leave you faith: faith in a power greater than yourselves who has gifted you mightily to love and love well, to love enough to overcome disdainful indifference; a faith the size of a mustard seed that can result in strength and communal connectivity the height of Mt. Everest; a faith that will give you hearts, spirits, and minds that are big enough to share with others, without needing to be competitive, punitive, jealous, or mean-spirited; a faith that you can believe in your communal and individual selves to plant a vision and make it real. I leave you love, faith, and hope so that you can and will "let your light shine" as audacious, engaging, awesome women, called to lead and excel for such a time as this.

Women, powerful
work, play, engage excellence
Your time is right now.

Part Two

Feminist Theologies
from Many Contexts

CHAPTER TWO

Pacific, Asian, and North American Asian Women's Theologies

Rita Nakashima Brock

TWO DECADES AGO, a group of Asian graduate students in religion formed Asian Women Theologians, which began a series of annual conferences for conversations among members of the organization. With the addition of a more diverse membership, including women from Canada, the organization settled on the name Pacific Asian North American Asian Women in Theology and Ministry (PANAAWTM).[1] PANAAWTM is now reaping the fruits of our program to help our members apply to doctoral programs and to mentor those seeking to become theologians and scholars.

THE FUTURE OF PANAAWTM THEOLOGY

The following is an extended excerpt from a 2005 statement on the future of PANAAWTM theology:[2]

> Although Asian and Asian North American women have different cultural, social and political contexts, our conversations in the past two decades have enriched and deepened understandings of diversity and

commonality among us. Facing the forces of globalization and the market economy, we recognize the need for continued dialogues and mutual challenges as we seek to examine how the global and the local are constantly reconstituted in the complex transpacific, hybrid, and intersected cultural and geographical spaces of our lives and our scholarship.

We recognize that both the terms "Asian" and "Asian American" are social and cultural constructs, arising out of particular historical stages of our political struggles. These terms have been useful for creating group identity and rallying support for political mobilization and for creating a space for our theological pursuits. They should not, however, be essentialized or homogenized so as to hinder critical reflections on diversity within our communities. We envisage there are at least six issues we need to address in our next decade as a grassroots organization.

First, PANAAWTM theology will continue to develop paradigms for religious life that affirm the value of our various cultures and multireligious environments. Our work is done in the aftermath of Christianity's involvement in colonialism, which changed the spirit of our peoples in many ways. It required us to deny our own traditions, to regard our multi-religious traditions and wisdom as demonic, to devalue our physical appearance as inferior, and to accept Western cultures and ideas as superior. Because of this colonial legacy in Asia and white racism in North America, the use of our cultural religious resources has not been emphasized in doing theology. Such Asian cultural resources have been available in English to Asian North Americans, but they have often been written with the gaze of colonialism, "orientalism," and racism, which has sometimes resulted in Asian North Americans avoiding Asian studies. Since the 1960s, when theological indigenization was espoused in Asia, the focus has been on the elite, male-dominated cultures of Asia, to the neglect of women's contributions. This Asian nativist approach has led to the homogenization of national cultures often according to one religious tradition, interpreted androcentrically. Furthermore, the use of a European definition of "religion" has created separate religious boundaries as if they are rigid and distinct.

Postcolonial theories point to hybridity as a way of conceptualizing porous religious, ethnic, and cultural boundaries. It should be clearly noted that the Christian movement has been hybrid and syncretistic from its beginnings, emerging from subjugated Palestine, where Judaism intersected with Greco-Roman cultures. Throughout its history, Christian thinkers and leaders have adopted and assimilated cultures and values of their own and of their neighbors. While we recognize the colonial legacy of Christianity in Asia in shaping our Christian feminist scholarship, we are also cognizant of our own backgrounds, interrogating not only Western Christianity but also constructions of gender and power in Asian religions and in Asian North America.

Second, in the spirit of radical inclusivity and of our awareness that diversity is our strength, we construct our theological understandings of human life attuned to the complexities of gender, race, culture, colonial history, class, and sexual orientation. This will require us to develop a theological anthropology that articulates a fluid and relational social self, a communal understanding of existence, and an embodied way of knowing as well as practicing religious life. From such a critical standpoint, we will be able to develop appropriate biblical and theological hermeneutics, both to interrogate the multiple experiences inscribed in the texts and oral traditions and to lift up the liberating potentials of our legacies. In striving to use multi-cultural, interdisciplinary methods for our scholarly work, we embrace the myriad forms of knowledge being created by new voices attuned to power, identity, history, and liberatory ideas and practices.

Third, we recognize bodies and sexualities as the nexus of power. Such power intersects with economics, politics, race, and intimate relationships, power both in the pain of domination and in the life-affirming possibilities of incarnation, the spirit in the flesh. Although we have challenged the sexual exploitation of women and children, sex industries and tourism, and "orientalized," sexualized stereotypes of Asian women, we are just beginning to develop a sexual theology, which affirms embodiment and sexuality. Such sexual theology will examine the intersections of colonization, racism, and homophobia in theories of human sexuality, as well as integrating elements from Asian traditions more tolerant of diverse sexual expressions. Hence, our theologies of sexuality will maintain a dialogue with Asian wisdoms, sexual stories, and experiences about the dangers and wonders of embodied life. In addition, this sexual theology will examine the relation between the private and the public in the construction of sexuality in our communities. Sexuality has often been seen as concerning the private or the familial realm, such that public discussions of it were discouraged. This construction has an ambivalent legacy: sexuality has not been so politicized and objectified, but this tends to silence diverse sexual expressions.

Fourth, we recognize diverse theological methods within our communities and in dialogue with other women and men who seek justice and wholeness for life. With such partners in the struggle, we develop new ideas of social selves, just relationships, healthy communities, and harmonious living with nature based on the deep spiritual resources of the many cultures in which we have been formed and to which we relate. In doing so, we will develop new methodologies of doing theology and of thinking about race and ethnicity beyond the either-or, white/other paradigms that have shaped racial relationships in North America and in the colonial imagination.

Fifth, we ground our new visions and hope in the importance of spiritual, religious, and pedagogical practices that affirm the gift of life and celebrate it in joy and gratitude. We create spiritual and ritual forms that ground us in material life while binding us with each other through respect of difference and mutual attunement to each other. This involves both the spirituality of perseverance, the ability to hold on when the road is tortuous, and the spirituality of letting-go, to accept the fragility and vulnerability of life. We develop pedagogical practices that empower others to search for their own wisdom and creativity, that create healthy communities of teachers and learners, and that provide means for Asian and Asian North American women to create their own communities of discourse and develop a field of thought called PANAAWTM theologies.

PANAAWTM theology is based on ancient wisdom in our traditions, which refuses either-or choices and seeks to live out an inclusive vision for life through a cultural logic that respects differences and celebrates diversity. Wisdom taps various cultural resources in constructing hope for a just world, while at the same time, living with a pragmatic sensitivity about life in every moment. We embrace a spirituality of joy, appreciation, and compassion that is alive in the midst of the struggle for justice.

We will continue to construct theology with mindfulness, courage, and hope, sustained by tenderness of heart and hard-won wisdom. We hope to create a foundation that others can build on for generations to come.

ASIAN NORTH AMERICAN FEMINIST THEOLOGICAL ANTHROPOLOGIES

PANAAWTM theologians have produced several treatments of christology, beginning with my 1988 book, *Journeys by Heart: A Christology of Erotic Power*. Christology is a central Christian theological category for discussions of anthropology, since the humanity of Jesus Christ is the form in which God is most in solidarity with human existence.

In 2002 Grace Kim published *The Grace of Sophia: A Korean North American Women's Christology*. Kim draws on four religious strands—the wisdom traditions of the Bible; Jewish and Christian traditions; the Buddhist idea of *prajna*, or wisdom; and Kwan Yin traditions of East Asia—to construct a christology based on the incarnation of wisdom and Sophia. In framing grace in terms of Jesus/*prajna* and Sophia/Kwan Yin, Kim suggests such grace is a source for Korean North American women of healing from *han*, of empowerment to resist injustice and to claim dignity, and of committed, intelligent action for others.

Wonhee Anne Joh, in her 2006 book, *Heart of the Cross: A Postcolonial Christology*, uses the lens of cultural hybridity to discuss human nature. By using the Korean cultural concept of *jeong*, Joh grounds her discussion of human anthropology in the inescapable nature of existence as fluid, complex, and relational. *Jeong* refers to the inevitability of relationships, both in their difficulty and intractability and in their necessity for human existence. Joh's description of *jeong* as "sticky" places her understanding of relationality counter to the firmly boundaried ego of the West, which tends to prefer Teflon relationships to sticky ones. Visually, I imagine the difference as a pile of bread rolls, side by side but loose, and a pile of rice balls, distinct but difficult to separate. Stacking rice balls changes the shape of the individual balls, and pulling them apart often involves bits from one ball sticking to another.

Joh offers us a theological concept, based in Korean culture, that is one of the richest I have encountered since Andrew Sung Park wrote *The Wounded Heart of God*, his book on *han*. *Jeong* describes a theological anthropology, a new way of thinking about human relationships, identities, and ethics that is, I would suggest, more accurate about human experience than the polarized dualisms characteristic of Western Christianity, which places opposites into mutually exclusive categories rather than seeing them as relationally interpenetrating and unstable. Her anthropology also runs counter to the Emersonian strains of individualism so characteristic of American ideas of self.

The theological subtext of all three of our christological works is incarnation. We discuss the nature of human selves in relationship as how we are incarnate in each other, just as the presence of God is in the world. Asian North American women's interest in the nature of human life as social and ontologically grounded in relationship is, I would suggest, prominent because questions of identity and selfhood are forced upon us by our cross-cultural, transpacific lives and our struggle for a postcolonial articulation of theology. In this struggle to construct selves as relational, complex hybrids of worlds, we emphasize a way of speaking about the healing, dignity, and power of Asian North American women.

This emphasis on incarnation can be developed into a theological anthropology using the ancient concept of *theosis*,[3] the process by which Christians, through the indwelling Holy Spirit, achieved the wisdom and power needed to become divine, that is, to incarnate the Spirit bequeathed to them by Jesus Christ through baptism. As Gregory of Nyssa put it, "Because our nature is mixed with the divine nature, our nature is made divine. . . . In the baptism of Jesus all of us, putting off our sins like some poor and patched garment, are clothed in the holy and most fair garment of regeneration."[4] According to his Alexandrian contemporary, Athanasius, "God became man so that we might become god."[5]

Virginia Burrus, in *Begotten, Not Made*, raises important cautions about the development of this idea of *theosis* in the post-Nicean, Constantinian church. The increasingly rigid and imperial bureaucracy necessitated more virulent forms of masculinity. Burrus notes, "When the confession of the full and equal divinity of the Father, Son, and Spirit became for the first time the *sine qua non* of doctrinal orthodoxy, masculinity was conceived anew, in terms that heightened the claims of patriarchal authority while also cutting manhood loose from its traditional fleshy and familial moorings."[6] Civic manhood and martyrdom were replaced by monastic models. Men began to groom for divinity via asceticism and a hyper-transcendental masculinity. Women, to overcome their carnal gender, were to be ascetic virgins. Despite these androcentric models, Burrus suggests that the concept of *theosis* might offer interesting theological directions deconstructed of its gendered biases.

Hints of a less sexist form of *theosis* are found in a theologian of the Nicean period, Ephrem of Syria. Like his contemporaries, Ephrem regarded the Incarnation as the central Christian truth, in which God bridged the ontological chasm between divinity and a fallen creation for the purpose of reconciliation and human salvation. Ephrem understood salvation in Christ as the deification of humanity. In contrast to Athanasius, however, Ephrem frequently reiterated the reciprocal relationship between the Incarnation and humanity's deification. He wrote, "The Most High knew that Adam wanted to become a god, so He sent His Son who put him on in order to grant him his desire. . . . He gave us divinity, we gave Him humanity."[7]

Ephrem was a noted poet and hymn writer, and he wrote many hymns for women's choirs. He composed a number of hymns about marginalized women, such as Tamar, valorizing their boldness and courage. He did not lapse into sexualizing or stigmatizing them. The Samaritan woman was a very popular figure in the early church. Of her, Ephrem wrote:

> Blessed are you, drawer of ordinary water,
> who turned out to be a drawer of living water. . . .
> Blessed is your perception that you disputed with
> your Lord.
> Your dispute shows that your heart was not
> contemptible. . . .
> For she answered and spoke as a learned one,
> as a disputant, yet modestly, . . .
> she was modest yet her head was high
> and her voice was authoritative.
> He alone labored with you and sanctified you,
> in order to be like His glorious Father,
> Who alone fashioned woman and sanctified her,
> and led her to Adam . . .
> as from [the Samaritan woman], therefore,
> our Lord arose in this town,
> for by her He was revealed there. . . .
> She is a type of our humanity
> that He leads step by step.[8]

This ancient language of ascent, nobility, and glory rubs against contemporary democratic sensibilities. Western people who struggle for justice are allergic to thinking in terms of status stratifications— we want equality for all, a level playing field, freedom to choose our own destinies. For many mainstream Christians today, humility and a commitment to human dignity mean seeing ourselves in "the least of these," those who struggle and suffer most in an unequal, oppressive world. Suspicious of power at the top, we find our solidarity with the powerless. We prefer the Christ who descended to the lowest humanity. When we level the playing field, we seek solidarity with the oppressed and downtrodden, a bedrock commitment of liberation theology.

Early Christianity flattened the field at its upward reaches. Everyone—slave, woman, emperor—began life anew at baptism. The descent of Christ to human form was so humanity could be lifted up to paradise. As Ephrem of Syria noted:

> You came down and became the Guide to the House of life,
> The Way to discipline, the smooth [Way] to the kingdom,
> And the Gate of entry. . . .
> Divinity flew down to rescue and lift up humanity.[9]

The Christian ascent to glory was undertaken by the entire community; the strong helped the weak, and all held each other accountable for their commitment to the struggle. The transfigured body of Christ was an image of the entire sanctified community. As the apostle Paul reminded the Galatian church, "There is no longer Jew or Greek, there is no longer slave or free, there is no longer male and female; for all of you are one in Christ Jesus" (Gal. 3:28). The church provided the opportunity for all to follow the pattern of Jesus, transfigured by the Spirit into divinity.

In a society acutely aware of status differences, the followers of Jesus believed he had raised up "the least of these," beyond even the highest emperor, rather than lowering everyone to the least. They did not subscribe to the idea that misery loves company. Misery should be relieved. Christ was healer and comforter to those who suffered just as the community assisted each other. Misery was the state of a person in excommunication and penance, not the sanctified state of Christian life. The early Christians were encouraged to aspire to what they desired, rather than descend to a status they sought to overcome. The church did not promise this new divine life as a faint hope but provided the means by which the committed could achieve it together.

Kwok Pui Lan notes that in relation to Western Augustinian anthropologies, Asian understandings of human nature are far more optimistic and positive. Rather than regarding the human condition as miserable in sinfulness, East Asian cultures regard being born human as a great honor and privilege, an achievement of great worth that carries responsibility for the cultivation of wisdom and moral virtue. This Asian Confucian and Buddhist sensibility parallels that of early Christianity and *theosis*. While such hierarchical Confucian values grate against feminist sensibilities of equality and mutuality, many human relationships retain an asymmetrical quality, with responsibilities differing with different roles—parent to child, teacher to student, older to younger sibling, and so forth. Wisdom comes from understanding differences in roles and the greater ethical responsibilities that come with greater status and power.

Teresa Yu, in a master's thesis she defended at the GTU in 2004, suggested that *theosis* is an especially healing and liberating understanding of salvation to offer women in situations of intimate violence. It provides them with a way to affirm their own worth and dignity and offers a basis from which to resist violence rather than acquiesce to it. It assures women that they and their children have great worth, which they have an obligation to protect.

Theosis takes a high christology, Christ in glory, and attaches it to a high anthropology, so that Christ is leader, teacher, and friend. Humanity, in its journey to divinity, followed its forerunner, whose life revealed the way to God, especially his nativity, baptism, transfiguration, and resurrection. Humanity, endowed with free will, was created by God and baptized into an exalted state reflective of God's own image and glory. Later, with atonement theology involving sinful humanity, a low anthropology alienated Christians from a high christology as Christ became the judge of sin.

Theosis, as the journey of humanity to divinity, is the work of *eros*—of our desire to draw near to God and of our love of beauty, truth, goodness, mercy, courage, and humility. Erotic power shapes the life of the soul, the quality of relationships in our communities, and our capacities to be generous with each other and the world. *Theosis* is a communal, spiritual, ritual, moral, and aesthetic attunement to life that Robert Wilken calls "seeing": "Seeing is never simply beholding something that passes like a parade before the eyes; it is a form of discernment and identification with what is known. What one sees reflects back on the one who sees and transforms the beholder. As Gregory the Great . . . put it . . . , 'We are changed into the one we see.'"[10]

The baptismal phrase "the bride of Christ" is, perhaps, an apt metaphor for the *eros* of incarnation, for the passionate embrace of life in the flesh, for the union of body and soul with Spirit, and for the power of love that binds human communities in relationship to God and each other. *Theosis* encompasses ethics and justice, but its final framework is aesthetic. It is a form of salvation that addresses the quality of all relationships in our lives not only for their justness but also for their beauty. It allows us access to aesthetic, sensual, and visual interpretive frames that teach a discipline of attentiveness to the world. Through such discipline, we encounter divinity outside our personal, subjective experience of mind or soul, an attunement to life that helps us to recognize spiritual power in our complex encounters with the world. Through *theosis* we are offered a discipline of the spiritual journey of the heart, a discipline of *eros*, of pleasure and joy that are part of wisdom, and a discipline of the power of community and communal ritual. In short, a route to the power of Presence in its fullest, most life-giving dimensions, in this world and on this earth.

CHAPTER THREE

Latinas Writing Theology at the Threshold of the Twenty-First Century

Nancy Pineda-Madrid

LATINAS BEGAN WRITING THEOLOGY as part of a long history of resistance that can be traced back several centuries. To this day we resist the compounding forces—social, religious, cultural, political, and economic—that render us silent and invisible. It was no fluke that Ada María Isasi-Díaz, one of the originators of Latina theology, began one of her first articles (in 1985) with the words, "How more invisible than invisible can you be? And yet there is a quality of invisible invisibility. . . . Invisible invisibility has to do with people not even knowing that they do not know you. . . . We are so irrelevant that the mind constructs needed to think about us do not exist. Society at large thinks of us as Hispanic and the majority of Hispanics think of us as women."[1] Today, I read these words and ask myself, how *far* have we come?

A LATINA ANGLE OF VISION: FEMINIST AND GENDER-CONSCIOUS THEOLOGIES

Latina theologies must be understood as a reflection and expression of a long history of Latina consciousness. This consciousness—or critical recognition—has repeatedly arisen from the lived experience of gender, culture, race, and class inequities, coupled with the lived experience of enduring faith. After reflecting on their lived experience, Latinas have come to expect more from life and have struggled to realize their dreams. A few historical examples will clarify my point.

Sor Juana Inés de la Cruz (1648–95) serves as example of an extraordinary woman who was painfully aware of how the traditional expectations for a woman (marriage and family) rendered other possibilities all but impossible. Sor Juana made the difficult choice to break with tradition. Fulfilling traditional expectations would have severely limited her time for reflection and intellectual pursuits. The writings of this Mexican intellectual genius reveal an amazing command of the most important works in the fields of literature, science, philosophy, and theology, among others. She entered a convent of the religious order of St. Jerome (the Hieronymites), seeking, in the Virginia Woolfian sense, "a room of her own." Even though male scholars of her day could not help acknowledging her brilliant, creative mind, eventually church authorities judged Sor Juana's brilliance repugnant for a woman. She resisted, claiming in her famous *Respuesta a Sor Filotea de la Cruz* that to suppress her intellectual work would be to defy God, who gave her intelligence for a purpose. In her own words, "One truth I shall not deny . . . is that from the moment I was first illuminated by the light of reason, my inclination toward letters has been so vehement, so overpowering, that not even the admonitions of others—and I have suffered many—nor my own meditations—and they have not been few—have been sufficient to cause me to forswear this natural impulse that God placed in me: the Lord God knows why, and for what purpose."[2] In this same *Respuesta*, Sor Juana cogently argued for the rights of all women to pursue scholarly work, whether theological or otherwise.[3]

Other examples can be found in the nineteenth century. Many Latina/o families living in the Southwest trace their history back more than five generations. For these, the North American experience began in 1848, the year that Mexico and the United States signed the Treaty of Guadalupe Hidalgo. This treaty ended the Mexican-American War and resulted in Mexico ceding to the United States what are today the states of California, New Mexico, and Nevada and parts of Colorado, Arizona, and Utah. For several decades afterward, few Latinas living within the United States had an opportunity to learn to read and write, and for the more fortunate, "education" focused primarily on enhancing domestic skills.

From a study of the oral histories of Latinas living in California, the Southwest, and elsewhere in the United States, one can discern a scant but unmistakable critical recognition of the social limitation placed on women. In her 1878 memoirs, California resident Doña María Inocencia Pico strongly objected to the operative social norm for marriage. Whenever very young girls were sought for marriage, they were customarily married off as if they were disposable property. Born in Mexico in 1893, New Yorker and literary writer María Cristina Mena wrote many short stories in which female characters resisted their socially subordinate position. Mena used these characters to reveal the absurdity of reducing women to objects of beauty.

In the late nineteenth and early twentieth centuries, New Mexico writers like Nina Otero-Warren (1881–1965), Cleofas Jaramillo (1878–1956), and Fabiola Cabeza de Baca (1884–1991) each chronicled the staggering loss of culture, language, land, and livelihood that resulted from the Treaty of Guadalupe Hidalgo (1848). Their work reflected a cultural and ethnic critical recognition, specifically, a painful awareness of the physical and institutionalized violence against the Spanish, the Mexican, and the Indio. This violence was precipitated by zealous Anglo Americans determined to profit from the racist socioeconomic systems concerned with the advancement of their interests and the privilege of whiteness. These women's writings likewise recognized the multiple ways in which women's contributions were minimized and women's roles slighted.[4]

In her effort to resist this racist, sexist system, Nina Otero-Warren became active in public life and worked tirelessly on behalf of women. Otero-Warren played an instrumental role in ensuring that the women of New Mexico secured the right to vote in 1920. And in 1922 she called into question New Mexico's strictly male, largely white political establishment by running for Congress.[5]

These are but a few among many examples that illustrate the long history of Latina consciousness and resistance. Many times throughout the course of history, Latinas have spoken out against the socially restricted role of women, and Latinas have confronted and resisted the forces that have attempted to render their humanity somehow lesser. Latina theologies are an attempt to interpret this history of Latina critical recognition and struggle. Failure to acknowledge this history of struggle leads to the erroneous and injurious view that Latina theologies emerged exclusively in reaction to the white women's movement, thought, and theology, and in reaction to Latin American liberation theology. While these have undeniably made their contributions, Latinas' own particular history of struggle has played as prominent a role in the development of Latina theologies.

The term *feminist* remains a contested term among a number of Latina theologians. There are Latina theologians who claim that feminism has been a vital concept in multiple Latin American women's movements for more than a century. Thus, since the term *feminist* bears significant historical weight within the context of Latin America and among U.S. Latinas, they argue that the term must *not* be viewed as a concept transplanted from white, first-world feminist, and women's movements. Therefore, to identify their writings as "Latina feminist theology" is entirely tenable. A large number of Latina theologians with a critical gender, race, and class consciousness subscribe to this view. However, the marker "Latina feminist theology" needs to be understood as reflecting quite diverse methods and sources. While these Latinas all attend to the particularity of Latina experience, what constitutes "Latina experience," how it is understood, and the methods of identifying it vary quite widely among these theologians. Consequently, their work reflects engagement with different disciplines to access "Latina experience." The disciplines range from philosophy to literature, from history to feminist theory, from sociology to postcolonial discourse, from critical theory to race theory, to name a few. The varied methods and sources used by these thinkers reveal a great deal of creativity but also a discourse in its initial, formative stage of development. Some of the thinkers writing in this area are María Pilar

Aquino, Jeanette Rodríguez, Michelle Gonzalez, Teresa Delgado, Nora Lozano-Díaz, Gloria Loya, and myself.

Other Latina theologians have adopted a different approach to writing theology. For these theologians the term *feminist* invariably means that sexism plays *the* primary role in every woman's experience of oppression and is defined by its association with middle- and upper-class white women of the first world. They see this association as rendering racism and classism secondary. Hence, these Latinas distrust the term *feminist* and name their experience of oppression using a term that they identify with the interrelated character of race/class/gender oppression. *Mujerista* (in support of Latina women) theology exemplifies this position. For *mujerista* theologians, the primary purpose of theology is to identify oppressive societal structures and to provide an impetus for both the transformation of these structures and the conversion of human beings. The experience of Latinas is foundational for *mujerista* theology, as is the way in which that experience is accessed. This discourse is distinguished by its use of the social sciences, specifically sociology, anthropology, and ethnography. Like all forms of Latina theology, *mujerista* theology employs several other disciplines as well. Theologians Ada María Isasi-Díaz and Yolanda Tarango have been at the forefront of developing *mujerista* theology. However, other Latina theologians have used the social sciences in their work in ways quite similar to self-identified *mujerista* theologians.

These various approaches to Latina theology have essentially the same goal—they seek the liberation of Latina women—but they differ in method; that is, they employ different sources and assign different priorities to the sources they engage.

EMERGING QUESTIONS:
THE SHIFTING CONTEXT OF
OUR THEOLOGICAL CONSTRUCTIONS

While Latina experience is, needless to say, quite diverse (including Mexican American, Puerto Rican, Cuban American, Guatemalan American, Salvadorean American, and so forth), in what follows I draw on the Mexican American, Chicana experience. In the southwestern region of the United States, this experience is predominant. *Chicana* here refers to Mexican

American women who possess a gender, race, and class consciousness.[6] *Latina* functions as an umbrella term to refer to women who reside in the United States and trace their roots to the countries of Central America, the Caribbean, Latin America, and Mexico. While all Chicanas may be considered Latinas, only a subsection of Latinas are Chicanas. Even so, Chicana theory has a long history and has much to offer Latina feminist theology.

As Latina theologians enter the twenty-first century, they face a wide range of questions. First, Latina theologians must continue to ask the question of identity and, relatedly, the question of subjectivity. As long as the full humanity of Latinas remains problematic, these questions will remain central.

Chicana feminist theorists have much to contribute to this investigation. In varied ways, they call attention to the notion of a "both/and" identity, an awareness of the contrasting, at times conflicting, dimensions of Latina/Chicana identity. Within the current discourse of U.S. Latina theology, this both/and identity has been named as *mestizaje* and as *mulatez*; however, the contributions of Chicana feminist theorists require that we consider this both/and identity anew. For example, the work of Gloria Anzaldúa suggests that fostering a *mestiza consciousness* enables Chicanas to name themselves and to boldly claim a space for themselves. Anzaldúa describes a *mestiza* consciousness as an oppositional feminist consciousness pointedly focused on deepening Chicanas' self-esteem by working to transform "the sexist elements in the Mexican-Indian culture," to affirm the equal dignity and power of men and women, and to enable Chicanas to act and not merely react as they live in this world.[7]

To begin with, according to Anzaldúa, Chicanas must leave behind the role of victim, that is, *la mujer sufrida* (the woman who suffers). She observes that "in the Chicano culture we grow up feeling it's a given that guys have all the power and privileges, that guys are more honest than women, that men aren't as competitive as women, that men don't gossip, and that men are more intelligent than women. . . . What's got to happen now is not concentrating so much on that kind of victimhood but concentrating on how we're liberating ourselves . . . as Chicanas."[8] Liberation comes through shedding the role of victim and affirming personal agency. But the development of an enhanced sense of personal agency is not an end in itself. Personal agency has value not only because it enables one to resist the destructive character of oppression but also, and more importantly, because personal agency is crucial if one aspires to work effectively toward change in society.[9] The new *mestiza*, engendered and affirmed in Anzaldúa's project, embraces her life as a rich tapestry of sharply contrasting threads. In some sense she is a polymorphous subject.

> The new *mestiza* copes by developing a tolerance for contradictions, a tolerance for ambiguity. She learns to be an Indian in Mexican culture, to be Mexican from an Anglo point of view. She learns to juggle cultures. She has a plural personality, she operates in a pluralistic mode—nothing is thrust out, the good, the bad and the ugly, nothing rejected, nothing abandoned. Not only does she sustain contradictions, she turns the ambivalence into something else.[10]

Chéla Sandoval puts forward a somewhat different approach. Today Chicana/Latina feminism is part of U.S. third-world feminism that concerns more than the creation of a "coalitional form of consciousness opposed to dominating powers and oppressive racial and social hierarchies," and more than a commitment to "racial, decolonial, and class liberation."[11] It concerns identifying with the notion of "third," meaning identifying with and being a force that serves to move through "dominant meaning systems" and break up "binary divisions of human thought."[12] As a result, disorder has become a central category for Chicana feminism thought today.[13] Disorder is a strategy of organized resistance, a strategy that fosters an oppositional form of consciousness so as to "ensure that ethical commitment to egalitarian social relations enter into the everyday, political sphere of culture."[14] Its aim is to equalize "power on behalf of the colonized, the nation-, class-, race-, gender-, and sexually subordinated."[15]

The contributions of Anzaldúa and Sandoval pose a challenge to the binary modes of conceptualizing that undermine Chicana humanity. The work of each suggests that the very bodiliness of Chicanas reveals a transcendental reality, namely that Chicanas are a third, are a "both/and." Chicanas, like all Latinas, live "life on the hyphen." Latina feminist theology would be well served by reflecting more critically on the significance of the "both/and" identity of Chicanas and all Latinas.

Second, Latina feminist theologians must continue to examine the relationship between sexuality and power. More particularly, if the full humanity of Latinas is a norm for theological discourse, then gendered symbols that bolster a patriarchal world of meaning must be analyzed, critiqued, and transformed. To the degree that these symbolic constructs have supported patriarchy, they have inevitably served to keep Latinas desexualized and thus less than whole. For example, the common symbol *la familia* carries with it an effective history that has denied the full humanity of Chicanas and consistently excluded some Chicanas and Chicanos judged to be culturally incorrect. The efficacious power of *la familia* is rooted in the deeply held communal, relational self-understanding of Chicanas. The idea of the "self" invariably means "self in community." Accordingly, the symbol *la familia* serves as a means by which Chicanas come to a greater self-understanding. It both reflects and forms identity. Therefore, how *la familia* is interpreted matters greatly, and who interprets *la familia* is of vital importance.

Chicana feminist theorist Cherríe Moraga has explored the effective history of this symbol. She observes that some Chicanas have questioned the short-sided boundaries of traditional, heterosexual interpretations of *la familia*. Traditional interpretations have served to undermine Chicanas committed to their full humanity because they have excluded and continue to exclude the validity of female sexuality in general. In addition, these interpretations exclude the reality of gays and lesbians. Moraga argues that all of these concepts of sexuality are relevant today.[16] Not surprisingly, her critique has brought on anti-*familia* accusations. Yet Moraga has persisted and offered more than a critique. She has put forward a countercultural vision of *la familia*, one in which Chicanas (and all Latinas) come together for the purpose of exploring and celebrating Chicana/Latina womanhood. Her vision responds to the challenge to imagine a community that genuinely supports the full humanity of women, one that fosters life-giving relationships among women so that they can be *la familia* for one another.

Third, and finally, Latina feminist theologians must fully understand and directly confront the challenge of their own binary systems of thought. As several feminist theorists have repeatedly shown, binary systems limit women's capacity "to be" in the world, to inhabit who they are. Although Chicanas' struggles with binary systems are, in some respects, similar to the struggles of other women, Chicanas, nonetheless, experience binary systems in a distinct way because these systems are filtered through a culture of honor and shame and because they function not only along gender lines but also along the lines of race and class. The compounded effect of these particularities creates an intensified and distinguishable experience for Chicanas and, arguably, all Latinas. Latina theologians need to better understand the dynamic effect of this complex experience.

One example of a binary system can be found when we turn our attention to interpretations of the Marian image of Guadalupe. Few would deny the potency of the symbol of Guadalupe, yet her efficacious support of the liberation of women cannot be easily assumed. The work of Chicana feminists makes this clear. Guadalupe, claims Chicana feminist theorist Norma Alarcón, must be understood in light of the binary pair of Malinche-Guadalupe that dominates the Mexican/Chicano oral and intellectual traditions on the subject of female symbolic figures. Malinche represents subversive, evil woman, while Guadalupe represents "transcendence and salvation." The Mexican/Chicano cultural tradition has used these female symbols as a means of reading and judging women and thus exerting control over their lives.[17] The origins of this binary pair reside in Mexico's nation-making process and thus in the development of a Mexican national consciousness.

This binary pair functions analogously to the biblical stories of Eve and the Virgin Mary, establishing a dualistic, Manichaean system of thought. Malinche-Guadalupe functions, says Alarcón, as contrasting markers of womanhood for the purpose of suppressing Chicana human agency by means of polarizing women. In Alarcón's words:

> Guadalupe's transcendentalizing power, *silence*, and material self-sacrifice are the positive, contrasting attributes to those of a woman who *speaks* as a sexual being and independently of her maternal role. To speak independently of her maternal role, as Malinche did, is viewed in such a society as a sign of catastrophe, for if she is allowed to articulate her needs and desires she must do so as a mother on behalf of her children and not of herself.[18]

Thus Guadalupe, in Mexican/Chicano culture, has become directly identified with a woman who fulfills her role as defined by traditional societies, that is, to produce members of the group who dutifully fulfill their place and function in society. Such a woman ideally teaches her children to be "good" members of society who in their thought and actions unwittingly support the patriarchal, colonial status quo. In such a society any woman who does not fulfill this function is viewed as subversive or evil, a "Malinche," if you will. Moreover, the fulfillment of such a traditional role operates in direct conflict with a woman's "creativity and inventiveness" and her desire to redefine herself in a manner more true to her "experience and vision."

These three emerging questions—that of identity and subjectivity, that of the relationship between sexuality and power, and that of the particularity of binary systems of thought—will be among the more pressing theological concerns of the twenty-first century.

THE GRADUATE THEOLOGICAL UNION AND LATINA THEOLOGY

As a consortium of nine independent theological schools and eight program centers, the GTU has been described as an umbrella without a handle—an apt description. The GTU needs to develop a handle. It not only needs a vision of the collective but substantial resources that will allow its leadership to act in decisive and bold ways in the name of the *whole* GTU community. The GTU needs to be better prepared to realize its vision of equipping leaders for a future of diverse religions and cultures. Such a vision must have Latinas and Chicanas at the center.

I ask, if not here at the GTU, then where? Where in these United States would it make better sense to realize such a vision? In the state of California, roughly half the population is either Latino/a, African American, Asian American, or Native American, and Latinos/as make up an overwhelmingly significant portion. California has a long history of Chicano/a/Latino/a studies programs with significant and substantial resources at the many campuses in the Bay Area and beyond. What other state and what other metropolitan area have the diversity of theological resources coupled with strong Chicano/a/Latino/a studies programs?

What other region of the country would be more ideally suited to take the theological education of Latinos/as seriously?

Even the land of California bears the marks of the long history of Latinas/os' gains and losses, a history that spans almost five centuries. The names we long ago gave it speak of an enduring Latino/a presence. Will the echoes of this land be heard at the GTU? The echoes are everywhere—found in the names of the twenty-one missions of *California norte* that link and distinguish it from the missions of *California sur*, the *baja*. The echoes are everywhere—found in the names of the cities of this state—San Francisco, San Diego, San Jose, Los Angeles, Sacramento. Will the GTU hear these echoes loudly and clearly, or will it follow the path taken by the California system of higher education? Just as the percentage of people of color has become roughly one-half of the state's population, California has chosen to decrease funding for higher education. Will theological education at the GTU remain the purview of those with money—excluding many capable Latinos/as? How will the GTU respond? It has been 330 years since Sor Juana Inés de la Cruz lived. While I have no doubt that if she lived today, she would be accepted into the GTU doctoral program. But I wonder, would the GTU make it financially possible for her to attend?

CHAPTER FOUR

Finding Questions and Answers in Womanist Theology and Ethics

Stephanie Y. Mitchem

WHY *WOMANIST?*

Womanist theology and ethics began developing in the mid-1980s in the United States. The discussions were inspired by a definition of *womanist* by black feminist Alice Walker. In four parts, it was styled like a dictionary definition, but in poetic language. Each section aimed to identify unique aspects of African American women, whether drawing from folk language—"You acting womanish"—or identifying black women as "universalist." Walker sketched a view of black women that incorporates race with gender. This definition was centrally important to African American women, who had long felt left out of feminist discussions and underappreciated in black liberation theological conversations. Walker wrote, "Loves the Spirit. Loves love and food and roundness. Loves struggle."[1] Such words as these spoke to aspects of black women's daily lives, pointing to a distinctive spirituality. Other words within the definition spoke to black women's sexuality, struggles for freedom, and concern for the wider community and for personal growth. The brief definition did not—nor was it meant to—say everything there is to say about black women.

While black women in other disciplines most often chose to use the term *black feminist* to describe their research, the term *womanist* was particularly freeing for African American women religious scholars. The word provided a new focus for research about African American women's experiences of faith and religion and a particularly helpful way to converse with black women in church communities that the word *feminist* never would achieve. In fact, the word *feminist* continues to alienate black women. The film *Mona Lisa Smile*, about women at Wellesley College in the early 1950s, provides an example of distances between white and black American women's experiences. The women in upper-crust Wellesley at that time were all white, and there were no black women in the school—there was, as yet, no legal end to Jim Crow America. The film's characters were preoccupied with marriage and fulfillment their wifely roles. The world portrayed in the movie clearly needed feminist thought, but that world and the related feminist analysis would necessarily have excluded black women.

When I was a student in the 1980s, the exclusion of black women continued. I remember one of the white women professors stating that the feminist movement helped women get out of the house. However, black women were not the cosseted, closeted creatures that patriarchy tried to make of white women. Black women were already out of the house, often taking care of those white women's houses. Differing social realities meant that black families' challenges were different. Yes, patriarchy had a solid grip on black women's lives. But there were many distinctions, especially in the ways that race and social class defined our black gendered lives as less important and more expendable than white women's lives.

The 1970s feminist movement ignored the distance between white and black women. The concept of "woman" was based on middle-class white women's identities. White women, while pushing for rights, sometimes appropriated the rights language of black people, with some women going so far as to call themselves "niggers." One black woman activist in the 1970s, Linda La Rue, stated, "It is time that definitions be made clear.

Black people are oppressed . . . white women are suppressed . . . and there is a difference."[2] While one might argue about her statement, her resentment is apparent. Around that same time period, Toni Morrison stated the distance between black and white women eloquently: "What do black women feel about Women's Lib? . . . Distrust. . . . Too many movements and organizations have made deliberate overtures to enroll Blacks and have ended up by rolling them. They don't want to be used again to help somebody gain power—a power that is carefully kept out of their hands."[3]

Yet there are important relationships between womanist and feminist work. Each group begins from the perspective of women and has the potential to support each other in significant ways. Both have developed in multiple directions with new expressions in different cultural frameworks. Both utilize forms of theology and ethics that deliberately include a focus on gender analysis. More women than those in the West use the term *feminism*, and, particularly today, global dialogues occur. Feminism and womanism are part of a continuum with distinctions of note; consequently, there is a range of womanist and feminist thought, approaches, and methodologies. For instance, two interesting types falling along the continuum are papal feminism and Africana womanism. Generally speaking, both of these forms ultimately analyze gender at the expense of women and *for* the benefit of men. But both would still locate themselves on the continuum of feminist thought. To presume that all feminist or womanist thought is the same creates essentialized categories.

Race, class, and gender were the definite starting points of womanist analysis since it began development more than twenty years ago. Alice Walker's definition was a catalyst, not a finished product. From the unique perspective of African American women's life experiences and social standings, the ethical analyses of race, class, gender, and other forms of oppression became foundations on which womanist theology was subsequently built. Five general features of a womanist ethical analysis can be identified.

First, womanist methodology may draw upon assorted social science tools as well as the works of other ethicists and therefore is interdisciplinary in approach. Because womanist ethics contributes to processes of writing black women's untold stories, multiple disciplines must be used. History, sociology, literature, anthropology, medicine, cultural studies, or political science may get blended with homegrown black philosophies springing from street sense and folk sayings. Such construction is not haphazard but calls forth a rigor of its own along with a willingness to become proficient in the languages of different disciplines.

Placing black women at the center rather than as marginal add-ons becomes indispensable to the foundations of both womanist ethics and theology. The womanist method of centering black women has been sharply critiqued by some white scholars. For instance, the womanist ethicist Katie Cannon has cited the criticism she once received: "African American women scholars are non-political." When she asked for clarification, the questioner responded, "'Well, it seems to me that womanist work is not talking about White people.' I said that is correct. We do not begin nor end our work with White people on our eyeballs. So he and others conclude that if Euro-Americans are not the focal point of departure then womanist work is without political significance."[4] Centering black women, particularly in using the term *womanist*, is critiqued by some feminists as well. Womanism, in these views, fragments feminism (although feminism has been fragmented from its beginnings) and avoids pushing black women to enter into the larger streams of feminist thought. But such thinking does not resolve the historical and present tensions, continues to avoid listening to black women, and constructs a kind of hegemony in feminist thought. The need to provide critical analysis that centers black women while dialoguing with women of all colors and political leanings is central in the ever-tightening net of globalization.

Centering black women is consequently the basis of the next four features of womanist ethical analyses. Womanist ethics, secondly, deeply analyzes the real social conditions that impact black women's materiality. The writings of womanist ethicists Joan Martin and Marcia Riggs are examples of this type of analysis: Martin analyzes black women and the world of work through enslaved black women's experiences;[5] Riggs critiques the black church's mistreatment of black women.[6]

The third feature is the historical grounding of womanist ethics, integral to its methodological focus, which draws from past black women's voices to relate them to current experiences. Joan Martin's book is an example of this approach. This focus does not mean that black women in the past were womanists. However, Sojourner Truth, Ida Wells Barnett, Zora Neale Hurston, and others provide a reflexive historical context that gives background on why black women think, respond, and react in the ways they do, as well as the basis of contemporary social conditions.

Fourth, distinctive relationships of black women to other groups, such as family, community, black men, and white men and women, are recognized and built into the ethical analysis. Finally, womanist ethics analyzes and draws upon the unique, embodied spirituality of black women. This spirituality also plays a significant role in the construction of womanist theology.

Womanist theology is closely linked with and draws from womanist ethical insights. The link between ethics and theology is parallel to that in other liberation theologies. Constructing theologies in the voices of those who are subjugated, marginalized, poor, or oppressed demands critical and reflexive analyses of their contextualized experiences. Why is this group subjugated? On the edges of what society are the marginalized? Who are the oppressors, and why? Who benefits from the current situation? What are responses to these experiences? Theological construction takes the next step by analyzing faith responses, critiquing shortcomings of organized religions, witnessing the values of the oppressed, and naming the holiness of life in impossible situations.

Womanist theologians use the tools of womanist ethics with those of multiple disciplines to comprehend and construct theologies from black women's points of view. Like other liberation theologies, womanist theology grasps the importance of culture, human experience, and lived faith, utilizing each as a location for religious analysis. With womanist ethics, womanist theology may serve to critique social systems and conditions that impact black communities. Womanist theologians recognize distinctive aspects of black women's spirituality and build theological constructs from the ordinary theologies of black women's lives. Further, by centering black women, new understandings of the meaning of doctrines, which had been imprisoned in white and/or male frames, can occur. These are the explorations of womanist theology.

Katie Cannon has concisely stated the ends of womanist thought:

> The chief function of womanism is not to replace one set of elitist, hegemonic texts that have traditionally ignored, dismissed, or flat-out misunderstood the existential realities of women of the African Diaspora with another set of Afrocentric texts that had gotten short shrift and pushed to the margins of the learned societies. Rather our objective is to use Walker's four-part definition as a critical method-ological framework for challenging inherited traditions for their col-lusion with androcentric patriarchy as well as a catalyst in overcoming oppressive situations through revolutionary acts of rebellion.[7]

Womanist ethics and theological constructions are grounded in the complex interconnections of race, class, and gender from black wom-en's points of view. Race-class-gender analysis, however, is not exclusive to womanist thought. Rather, this analysis served as the beginning point of black feminist analysis and is reflected in the title of the classic 1982 text *All the Women Were White, All the Men Were Black, But Some of Us Were Brave*.[8] The black feminist analytical approach continues and is one with which womanists dialogue and to which we contribute. Naming ways that African American women have understood race, class, and gender within the context of religious life is a specific womanist contribution to the wider dialogue among liberation scholars. Womanist ethicists and theologians go beyond analysis to create theological statements, chal-lenges, and constructions that remain centered on black women's lived realities. To clarify, I will now briefly describe some aspects of womanist discussions of race, class, and gender.

RACE

The construction of race has shifted in the past fifty years, but race remains, as black feminist historian Evelyn Brooks Higginbotham termed it, a *metalanguage*. Toni Morrison baldly stated the truth of the matter when she wrote, "I have never lived, nor has any of us, in a world in which race did not matter."[9] Some scholars today would prefer to forgo racial analysis, hoping that silence will make it go away. But racial issues are complex and global, demanding more thorough analysis rather than denial or valorization.

Race continues to colorize American perceptions, and this is especially true for black women. What feminine ideal of beauty is promoted in the United States? Do images of female beauty exclude black women unless we look, act, and sound like a mythologized version of white women? Are black women still perceived as Jezebels, mammies, or Sapphires? These become questions in womanist theology when thinking about God and Christian anthropology. If we are all made in God's image, and black women are somehow flawed, then what does that mean? These questions surface repeatedly in some form exemplified by media discussions of well-known black women, such as Oprah's weight, the Williams sisters' clothing, Halle Berry's love life, or Janet Jackson's morality. Similar questions are asked more quietly in terms of poorer black women who are deemed "welfare cheats" or "crack heads." These images are powerful, supporting that all-American sport, the constant surveillance of black women.

CLASS

Awareness of class constructions is most important because it provides the context for comprehending race and gender in nonessentialist ways. Analyzing African American women's roles and realities becomes a strategic stance from which to view class structuring in black communities because we can consider unquestioned categories and underlying beliefs. Class stratifications in black communities today have reached new levels of sophistication and complexity. The categories of race and ethnicity are sometimes defined as abstractions that can set up the denial of the existence of racism. Integration, such as it is, seems to indicate that distributive justice might just be possible. However, African American households generally lost income between 2000 and 2001. Despite economic gains, from 2000 to 2001 a nagging $15,000 gap between African American and white median incomes in all households remained. Since income alone is not the sole determinant of wealth, how equal is opportunity for African Americans in the United States?

Other questions are woven into the income gap. What does it mean to make a living as an African American in the United States? In African American communities, what is the level of access to services and goods? Do institutions—from banks to schools—block black community and personal growth? Are African American communities still redlined? How do these lived experiences impact the quality of life?

The majority of African American women continue to have lower incomes, lesser job opportunities, and greater stress. Marcia Riggs, a womanist ethicist, presents a stinging analysis of class stratification in her development of black liberationist concepts.[10] She explores the crisis wrought by acceptance of the values of a consumer society as black people struggle to enter or stay in middle-class income brackets. Riggs charges that as long as they are driven by consumerism, black Americans will remain conflicted in our ability to be moral agents.

GENDER

Black women, as mentioned earlier, are constantly under surveillance. One major area in which they are judged is gender. Are we acting like "ladies"? Are we being "good" women? In religious circles, this judgment is particularly brutal, as many churches construct their ideas of virtuous women based on a few lines in the book of Proverbs. Getting and keeping a man becomes another measure by which black women are judged within black communities. Who is responsible for the breakup of black women's marriages? Who is responsible for the rate of unmarried, single black women? Who is responsible for any black man's lack of success? Who is to blame for social and emotional problems of those sons of single black mothers? Black women are often cast as villains, solely responsible for all ills, without recognition of the contexts of American society or black communities. With this kind of press, African American women themselves sometimes embrace the blame for black social problems. They are then caught in the need to constantly prove themselves, driving themselves to do more and to achieve great things in any situation. Too much of African American women's gendered roles revolve around being able to "take it" (whatever "it" is) and keep on going.

In a no-win scenario, black women are also critiqued for being too strong, castrating, unfeminine, or unsupportive. These critiques are not only from African American men but from other black women. A powerful question for reflection posed for African American women during retreats has been, "When did you know you were a woman?" Repeatedly, black women have reported that learning to say no to the demands of everyone else was a critical factor in determining their own gendered identities. These women reported the painfully learned lesson that the fate of "the race" of black peoples did not hinge on whether or not they took time for themselves.

GROWTH AND EXPANSION

With Walker's definition and a toolbox from liberatory thinkers, womanist theology and ethics are rooted in the unique experiences of African American women. Womanist scholars in theology and ethics also deliberately remain connected to black communities, particularly in terms of their religious dimensions. Renouncing injustices experienced by black women in their church communities is part of womanist analysis. Some womanist scholars take active roles in their church communities—some experiencing tension between ministerial and academic roles, some having to choose one over the other. For instance, when womanist scholars remain connected to black women in communities, presenting talks or retreats in local congregations, in this day of neoconservative affiliations of some black churches, what might happen? Might the message get watered down or altered to sound like something the women members regularly hear from pulpits? To continue developing womanist theology and ethics will demand courage of black women.

Womanist activism also takes place in seminary settings. I gave a talk at a historically black seminary, where the black women students used womanist ideas to influence one of the men students. He reported to me that he had been opposed to womanist thought in the beginning but through the persistence of the women he had come to a new understanding. He said that he would now—legitimately or not—call himself a womanist.

Like the story of the seminary students, the dialogues between black women and men scholars of religions have led to some shifts in black theological constructions. Black liberation theologian James Cone stated the history of these dialogues in this way: "Womanist theologians broke the monopoly of black male theological discourse. They challenged the male advocates of black theology to broaden their narrow focus on race and liberation and incorporate gender, class, and sexuality critiques and themes of survival and quality of life in our theological discourse."[11]

Womanist thought in religion is not exclusive to black women who are Christian. Ariska Razak is a womanist scholar and activist who views Walker's definition as pointing away from Christianity. Razak's work in healing and midwifery is more related to nature-based religion, emphasizing a portion of Walker's definition that names a womanist as "universalist." Debra Mubashshir Majeed, who is Muslim, is an African American religious scholar. Majeed has begun to state womanist thought from an Islamic perspective.

Womanist scholars in the United States are also engaging dialogues and forging new alliances with black women throughout Africa and the African diaspora. Some of these dialogues are informal, some made possible through mutual research interests or conferences. This aspect of womanist work is only beginning.

Womanist thought in religion is no longer limited to black women in the United States. Lee Miena Skye is an Australian aboriginal woman. She completed her dissertation for the University of Sydney in 2005, "Documentation of Australian Christian Womanist Theology." For Skye, womanist theology is important because it allows women to write against the effects of colonization, giving a framework for liberation. She stated that race, class, gender, and naturism (abuse of nature) are important to deconstruct for the Australian context. Skye's work follows that of Anne Pattell-Gray, another aboriginal theologian who introduced womanist concepts to Australia. Womanist concepts in global conversation will certainly continue.

The twenty or so years of the development of womanist ethics and theology are not enough for its complete expression. The processes of developing womanist theology and ethics are firmly grounded in the lived experiences of black women and families, and these material realities have not remained static. The changing times have created a climate in which womanist analysis is particularly needed.

Despite the real or imagined advances of African Americans since the profound social and legislative activism of the civil rights movement, black people still experience marginalization in multiple forms of oppression in the United States. The bright hopes of the 1970s have instead become a grim world driven by greed and imperialism. Black people are still told to pull themselves up by their bootstraps, while new codes keep them in place. There is high talk about the "undeserving" poor and the "underclass" as irresponsible slackers, talk that claims to be race-free, but the mental image is of black, crack-addicted welfare mothers bringing street thugs into the world. Race, gender, and class are not discussed but dismissed as irrelevant in an American equal-opportunity fantasy. In this climate, womanist theology and ethics continue to evolve. Today, womanist analysis is particularly needed.

For instance, womanist thought has come to incorporate more than race, class, and gender as analytical windows, such as disability discrimination (ableism) and ageism. One of the current strands of research has been on the topic of black women's sexuality. Kelly Brown Douglas's book *Sexuality and the Black Church*[12] became one of the first extended studies of the difficulties of black sexuality in light of religious life. She named a white legacy of sexual assault that is in need of a black sexual discourse of resistance. This discourse would do more than stand against stereotypes of black sexuality. Black churches would also have an important role to play in reconnecting sexuality and spirituality, while combating heterosexism and homophobia.

Douglas wrote her text in 1999, but the conditions at this time make her call for a discourse of resistance even more urgent. Many black churches have been hijacked by the delusion that one political party in the United States is for God and the other is not, because one party combats gay marriage. The emphasis on opposing same-sex marriage shores up all forms of homophobia in black churches and eliminates any in-depth discussion of black sexuality. Sexuality and related gender roles become limited to white, Anglo-Saxon, neoconservative evangelical definitions. Twenty-first-century black church women's proper roles have come to mirror those of nineteenth-century Victorians, as black men sink deeper into patriarchy—and all of this flies under a biblical flag. Acceptance of these ideas occurred without reflection. As a result, there is tremendous dissonance in a people who claim to want *their* justice (for black men) but are unwilling to offer the same rights to others.

The problems around sexuality are not just evident in the presence of black homophobia and heterosexism. The reality of the spread of AIDS in black communities, particularly among black women, indicates that there are some real problems. Some black churches have begun to participate in the annual "Week of Prayer for the Healing of AIDS." This participation is a step in the right direction. However, the programs I have attended only discuss AIDS as transmitted by the sharing of needles among drug users. Somehow, discussions of drug addiction have become preferable to discussions of sexuality. Nevertheless, AIDS is spread through an exchange of bodily fluids, and the growing number of black people infected are not necessarily needle-using drug users or individuals associating with them. The inability to name sexuality and sexual practices in black communities indicates a dangerous ignorance and stresses again Douglas's call for a discourse of resistance. Sexuality has created a tremendous need for womanist analysis.

Economic questions of the twenty-first century are particularly pressing when the gap between the haves and have-nots continues to widen; African Americans are not the major beneficiaries of the current system. Social systems that were created to assist poor and minority Americans are now viewed politically as merely giving handouts to the irresponsible while taking money from righteous, hardworking taxpayers. These systems have included the much-maligned welfare and affirmative action programs but encompassed other programs for mental and physical health, job training, and child care. Meanwhile, jobs dry up, and all costs, especially those of health care, continue to rise. Black women—with high numbers of single mothers, the elderly, and the ill—become the ones most likely to be left without financial resources, even while they are often the ones who struggle to hold families together. At the same time, costs of higher education are rising, and access to financial aid is tightening, while the number of African Americans in prisons is increasing. All this is accompanied by media campaigns that blame the victims.

In one of my classes a young black woman became agitated when thinking about the needs for social justice in our current globalized context and complained, "This is not fair! Who's left for us [African Americans] to exploit?" Unfortunately, she wasn't joking. Young African Americans often want to participate in the fullness of American wealth, and too often they look to the Paris Hiltons and Donald Trumps as role models. How is holiness defined under these socioeconomic conditions? The reality of black people's lives needs more analytic attention from womanist ethicists and theologians.

Particular questions arise among African American women about womanist thought. The womanist concept continues to be refined by these internal dialogues. For instance, some women are still torn between the terms *womanist* and *black feminist*. This is a healthy tension because better definitions of both terms will most likely result. Other conversations result because some younger African American women scholars did not experience the struggles of civil rights, feminist, or Black Power movements. The world in which they have grown up has provided them with greater opportunities and choices. So why should they be concerned with womanist ideas? The annual Womanist Consultation, held prior to the annual meeting of the American Academy of Religion, has been helpful in stimulating dialogues about these and other related issues.

This brief examination of the challenges and questions of womanist theology and ethics is not exhaustive. I have named only a few womanist ethicists and theologians who have struggled with the multilevel dynamics that are involved. Dialogues within black communities, among African American women, and with other feminists and liberation scholars continue, and this will only strengthen all our work.

The scholarly foci of womanist, black feminist, feminist, and liberationist thinkers together provide important critical analyses drawing from multiple cultural traditions. Womanist theology and ethics form a layer in liberationist thought, seeking answers from its own scholarly stance, answering questions that are raised in black women's voices. These questions are old, having surfaced from the past, and they are new, arising from current conditions. After twenty years, womanist theology and ethics have only begun.

CHAPTER FIVE

Unfinished Business: The Flowering of Feminist / Womanist Theologies

Mary E. Hunt

THE TRANSFORMATION OF the Center for Women and Religion into an academic program of women's studies at the Graduate Theological Union is a continuation of the legacy of hundreds of women whose contributions have shaped theological education at the GTU since its founding in 1962. It represents the still-unfinished business around the world of changing patriarchal, racist, colonialist theological education into pedagogy for faith-inspired justice.

I arrived at the GTU in the fall of 1974, fresh from a master's degree at Harvard Divinity School. I was looking for a place to ask new questions, to explore what was then uncharted territory—feminist and liberation theologies. I recall vividly my first few days in Berkeley. I chose to live in a dorm, sight unseen, at the Church Divinity School of the Pacific (CDSP) because the first Episcopalian women, the "Philadelphia Eleven," had been ordained irregularly that summer. I mistakenly thought that CDSP would be a hotbed of feminism.

In search of same, I went to what was then the Office of Women's Affairs (a name later changed to protect the guilty, as we often joked).

I encountered the director, Sally Dries, and asked her two questions: what the GTU had to offer me as a woman, and where I could swim. She started with the easy one and pointed me in the direction of the outdoor pool at the Hearst Gym on the University of California campus in Berkeley. Then we began a conversation that for me has turned into a lifelong concern.

In those days, we were asking, Given millennia of discrimination, what could Christian theological education offer women? Answering that question eventually developed into what women need to do to make theological education tolerable and useful for our purposes. Gradually, what began as a white, Christian conversation became many conversations with diverse voices and faith traditions. Now the question is how a wide range of religious traditions are being shaped by women's religious experiences on women's terms. We are focused on what theologies will result and, more important, how the world will be more just because of it.

There is no doubt that women have made enormous strides in the thirty-five years that CWR and other women's projects in religion around the country and the world have been working. But there is equally no doubt that we have an enormous amount of what I think of as "unfinished business." The term brings to mind early CWR (then OWA) board meetings, in which activists like feminist theologian Anne McGrew Bennett and institutional representatives like GTU's longtime beloved registrar, Betty Over, moved the agenda like the good church women they were, checking off items as they made progress but always conscious of the "unfinished business." Successive generations simply pick up that agenda.

Examples of unfinished business for women in religion abound. In the name of interreligious politeness, I select one close to my Catholic home to illustrate my point, confident that there are myriad examples from other traditions of unfinished work, unaccomplished goals for women in religion that will orient future efforts. One of CWR's reasons for being was to promote and support women in ministry. Thirty-five years later, fully one-third of the GTU member schools (the Jesuit, Franciscan, and Dominican institutions) are part of a denomination, the

Roman Catholic Church, that still does not ordain women or, of more importance, permit women to make decisions about finances, sacraments, theological teaching, and the like. None of these three schools has distinguished itself in pushing a feminist agenda, although it is questionable if any one of them would still be open if they had no women students as paying customers. That is unfinished business, along with many other dimensions of feminist work in religion that theological education simply cannot ignore. I conclude that either CWR's reason for being remains more important than ever, or any new academic program proposed to fill the need to which CWR pointed must have an explicit feminist/womanist advocacy component.

To encourage such a program, I offer the following:

(1) a brief appraisal of what feminist/womanist work in religion has accomplished and failed to accomplish;

(2) future horizons in the work as I envision them from a white, Christian, lesbian feminist starting point;

(3) a description of how a program in feminist/womanist studies in religion in a seminary and university-based institution like the GTU might seek to achieve the goals of equality, justice, and solidarity that I take to be the impetus behind CWR, goals I consider more urgent today than when CWR was founded.

A brief appraisal of what feminist/womanist work in religion has accomplished, and perhaps more important, what it has failed to do, is necessary to situate this analysis. With the deepest respect for our foremothers and ourselves, I think it is fair to say that we have done seed work and begun to see the first buds of feminist/womanist work in religion but that the full flowering is still generations away. I say this for three reasons. First, feminist/womanist work in religion has transformed the intellectual landscape for feminists and womanists but has had relatively little impact on the field as a whole. The operative word is "relatively" of course, since in 1970 CWR's founders could not have envisioned the enormous production of knowledge and its application that feminist/womanist scholars have contributed. Rosemary Radford Ruether's dozens of books alone have changed the way we look at religion.[1] Hundreds of other colleagues have reread church history, reimagined scripture, rethought ethics, reshaped theology, recast liturgy and ritual, refocused pastoral relations, and reconfigured the pluralistic religious landscape in creative and constructive ways that reflect women's experiences on women's own terms. Much remains to be done in all of those fields, but the seeds are sown.

Nonetheless, many theologians and theological schools, not to mention churches and other religious institutions, remain either virulently opposed to incorporating such insights into their curricula or blissfully ignorant of the ways in which they need to change in light of such knowledge. Journals and scholarly meetings untouched by such concerns abound. With notable exceptions like the *Journal of Feminist Studies in Religion*, *Feminist Theology*, *Schlangenbrut*, *FAMA*, *In God's Image*, *Der Apfel*, *Conscience*, *Conspirando*, *South of the Garden*, and *WATERwheel*, among others, and certain sections of professional organizations focused on women's issues, the academic mainstream remains largely untouched by the depth of our agenda. This is unfinished business.

Rhetoric of the religious right is far more common especially as one moves beyond theological education. A good place to gauge progress is in the civil religious arena. Recall, for example, the worship service held in Washington, D.C., in the wake of the events of 9/11. President George W. Bush all but declared war from the pulpit of the National Cathedral in a service that featured male, bellicose language, imagery, and intent unnuanced by feminist/womanist anything. The only woman participant (besides the requisite female singer) was Bishop Jane Holmes Dixon, who was referred to by National Public Radio as "James." She happened to be the Bishop Pro Tempore of the Diocese of Washington, or there would have been no woman in the service whatsoever.

I would write this off as another vestige of old Texas conservatives if it were not for the fact that we face the same problem in the religious left, where so-called progressive men like Jim Wallis and Michael Lerner persist in dismissing, marginalizing, or ignoring feminist/womanist concerns, such as reproductive health, as integral parts of a progressive agenda. Many religious feminists/womanists are tired of begging for recognition or being instrumentalized when included in their projects. Plans are afoot to build our own women-led movements since we continue to have so little impact on the style and content of priority setting and decision making of so-called progressive religious men. The muddled middle has at most a passing acquaintance with our work, despite our best efforts to promote it in the popular arena. The bottom line is that while we are increasingly sophisticated in our analysis and differentiated in the nuances of our positions, our impact on the religious/cultural whole remains marginal relative to what it can and should be. This is especially true in the area of religious education, where precious little feminist scholarship is reflected in materials for children and young people.

A second reason I say that the full flowering of feminist/womanist work in religion is ahead of us is because there are very few places to study and train in the field, something that bodes ill for our future. Until we have a variety of programs and departments to which we can direct future graduate students, I fear that even the gains made by the pioneers may soon be eclipsed.

With all due respect to those who are teaching and writing in the field, I am hard pressed to cite five programs to which I could direct a potential graduate student and be sure that she would study a curriculum infused with feminist/womanist material, where her interest in goddess/pagan questions would be addressed with skill and without bias, and where her training for ministry would be women-centered with a healthy critique of kyriarchal institutions. I know this from experience with a recent summer intern at WATER, the Women's Alliance for Theology, Ethics and Ritual. Of course, at several major institutions like the GTU, Union Theological Seminary, Harvard Divinity School, and Chicago Theological Seminary, among others, she would find some courses and a few professors. But there is still virtually no school, much less any cluster of schools, that stands out as the premier, go-to place for feminist/womanist work in religion. In fact, at many schools she would meet more resistance than welcome.

This lack is the result of structural reasons: (1) the increasingly conservative and fundamentalist tide in many Christian denominations, which in turn is reflected in their institutions; (2) the backlash against feminist/womanist activism that has been an integral part of the theological project (for example, exclusive language and imagery that remain largely unchanged; undue focus on abortion and homosexuality as ethical priorities to the exclusion of focus on war, ecocide, and economic and racial injustice); and (3) funding priorities in hiring, research grants, and curriculum development that favor the status quo over challenges to it. While we have successfully raised issues and established intellectual watermarks, we have been thwarted regularly at attempts to change the theo-political structures that undergird the field.

As a result, people and projects are isolated. For example, a whole generation of intellectual pioneers, including Judith Plaskow, Carol P. Christ, and Rita Gross, has not been hired to teach in research universities; thus they are not training the next generation of graduate students. What a loss! There is also the systematic exclusion of Catholic feminists, including Rosemary Radford Ruether, Elisabeth Schüssler Fiorenza, and Margaret Farley, from Catholic faculties, so that their direct influence is unavailable to the next generation of Catholic students. While that loss is surely a gain for the rest of us, imagine the difference if Catholic institutions, including the three at the GTU, were to promote feminist/womanist work by Catholic women of such stature.

The same factors are at play in the history of independent women's organizations, many of which have come and gone over the years. The Immaculate Heart College Center offered an innovative master of arts degree in feminist spirituality. It is now defunct. The Ecumenical Women's Center in Chicago is gone, with no replacement in sight. The National Council of Churches recently defunded their Justice for Women staff person. The Church of the Brethren women's publication ceased recently, as did *Daughters of Sarah* several years ago, and even *The Other Side* magazine, which picked up the *Daughters of Sarah* subscribers, is now out of business.

Some may argue that such projects served their purpose and their demise makes way for new work to emerge. In my view, they are victims of these economic and ideological times, when the concerns of women and their dependent children are simply not a priority. At a time when economic injustice and war reign, we need our own resources more than ever, not principally for ideological reasons but to help achieve safety and survival for those who are marginalized by unmasking the religious components of oppression and proposing liberating religious alternatives.

The third reason I claim that we have unfinished business and that the full flowering of feminist/womanist work is ahead is because much of the work to date has reflected the context in which it was begun, namely hegemonic, white, Christian, colonial, heterosexist, xenophobic conditions that are subject to deconstruction. The frank fact of the matter is that thirty years ago women like me were slow to realize the extent of our own privilege—economic, racial, religious, and national. We were unclear about the degree to which we were products of mindsets and frameworks that limited our views—most of us were Christian, many heterosexual, many from the United States or Western Europe. We had to learn, often the hard way and at the expense of others, how and why in our struggles for justice for ourselves we were obligated to extend concern, analysis, resources, and energy to women and children—and minority men—whose very survival was and remains in the balance.

Today's context allows no such ignorance and admits no such ambiguity. The stakes are simply too high. Moreover, we know too much now about how religious images and symbols, beliefs and practices interact in the public forum to excuse any lapse in solidarity. Women around the world, and especially women of color in the United States, are naming and prioritizing their own theo-political agendas, which white, Western, Christian women like me learn from and collaborate with as respectful colleagues. However, we are still far from having eliminated the power imbalance. The kyriarchal dimensions of racism, economic domination, heterosexism, and colonialism and the hegemony of fundamentalist Christianity remain stubbornly in place.

For this reason, it is distressing to see one trend in feminist work in religion moving toward a postmodern theoretical discourse that eschews any explicit value claims. The nexus of theory and theology is, in my view, far too vexed and fraught with layers of meaning and implication, far too connected with the prevailing powers to leave the matter of morals in abeyance. Another trend in religion, welcomed by those who consider feminist/womanist work too political, is toward "woman-centered" work, "the feminine," and "partnership," as if two complementary halves make a whole. These efforts, while recognizing that women need attention, miss the theo-political points: namely that gender is only one piece of the puzzle and that concern for gender without an explicit feminist commitment to the well-being of women and children can be a grand distraction.

Many women shy away from the word *feminism*. I want to suggest that they do so at their peril—and mine. The word *feminism* means many things to many people. Most agree that it involves the radical notion that women are equal to men. Such language may sound antiquated, just a step away from women's suffrage. Would that it were the case. A look at how feminist work and discourse evolved shows that it was focused primarily on gender rights until womanist (African American), Asian, and *feminista/mujerista* (Latin American) colleagues insisted that survival issues were at stake: survival of women and dependent children, survival of whole communities, including men. These insights and the hard work that they signaled changed feminism forever. Commitments to eradicate racism and colonialism, to eliminate heterosexism and transform economic and ecological injustices, are now constituent parts of feminist agendas. Gender-exclusive white feminism is and ought to be dead.

Twenty-first-century feminism that takes gender issues as part of a complex interweaving of oppressions, what Elisabeth Schüssler Fiorenza has coined "kyriarchy," is alive and well as a critical analysis and strategy for bringing about justice.[2] As such, it is an understandable threat to those who want to roll back gains made by women, people of color, and others who have been marginalized, or at least to keep those gains from increasing. Part of that strategy is to declare feminism over, but it won't work as long as we acknowledge that injustice remains.

This leads me to suggest three future horizons for our work as I envision them from a white, Christian, lesbian starting point: diverse identities, diverse religions, and diverse sexualities.

I welcome and encourage the diversity that has broadened the question from its white, Christian starting point to a now multiracial, multiethnic, multireligious global project. While I reject false universals, I am, at the same time, wary of an identity politics that can divide and conquer rather than unite and build. At a historic first meeting of U.S. Latinas and feminist theologians from Latin America held in Mexico City in the summer of 2004, this delicate balance seemed to have been achieved. The conference report of the First Interamerican Symposium on Feminist Intercultural Theology states: "As a constant element, the group stressed the need of shifting our concerns from the restricting and limiting rhetoric of 'identity politics' to approaches that express the mobility and dynamism of the new social subjects in the global contexts lived today."[3] Note that this insight came from women who were indeed meeting on their own terms, with their own colleagues, so there is no suggestion that such identity work is unimportant—simply that it is not sufficient.

This realistic view welcomes all women as protagonists or agents of our own transformation on our unique terms. It recognizes that it is by commitments and not simply by identities that we function. I have learned, for example, that every white, Christian lesbian does not necessarily share my commitments to eradicating injustice. Such an approach that moves beyond identity politics is not an excuse to enshrine the same people and perspectives. Rather, it is a way to move forward with people who are willing to share the fruits of their work in the service of social change, always incorporating more and "new social subjects" who are working with the same commitments.

I think of this in relation to the intergenerational work we are doing at WATER. We who are over fifty learn from young women what they prioritize and value. In turn, we offer historical information and insights from our perspectives. Likewise, WATER's long-standing collaboration with colleagues in Latin America has taught me that women's voices emerge on their own terms and that my job is to learn the languages and listen. I respectfully suggest that this is how white, privileged people best acknowledge "the mobility and dynamism of the new social subjects in the global contexts lived today."

The feminist/womanist challenge in the United States is how to live religious pluralism despite continued persistent Christian hegemony.

In Christian theological education, pluralism begins on a practical level, namely how to have enough multireligious courses when budgets and ideologies are so strained that only the most orthodox Christian materials are taught. In the university setting, pluralism means having conversations about religion without assuming that those who are explicitly religious are in the business of proselytizing. Part of our unfinished business is to engage scholars, beginning with our women's studies colleagues who sometimes reject or shy away from colleagues in religion for fear that we are not intellectually rigorous or objective about our field. Their skepticism about kyriarchal religion is well founded, but our activist scholarship and our well-informed engagement in their disciplines will go a long way toward changing that stereotype.

Diana Eck, director of the Pluralism Project at Harvard, provides a useful framework for living in a religiously pluralistic society. She writes, "Pluralism is not diversity alone, but the energetic engagement with that diversity. . . . [It] will not require just tolerance, but the active seeking of understanding." Pluralism "is not simply relativism. . . . [It] does not require us to leave our identities and our commitments behind, for pluralism is the encounter of commitments."[4] It is this "encounter of commitments" that I think distinguishes feminist/womanist work from the many ill-fated patriarchal efforts at ecumenism and exercises in religious misunderstanding.

The Pluralism Project recognized the need for such an encounter and set in motion the Women's Networks in Multi-Religious America to bring together a new constellation of religious leaders. They did not simply invite the "obvious" institutional representatives. Rather, they sought out groups like the Jewish Orthodox Feminist Alliance, the North American Council for Muslim Women, and WATER to assure that the many traditions were represented by those who are pushing feminist/womanist horizons within their own communities.

Our several meetings have been rich beyond description. I cannot forget Jewish and Palestinian women in heated plenary conversation only to say to one another over lunch, "What is it you want me to do?" Both modes were taken seriously. During the 2004 campaign season, many of us met at the National Press Club in Washington to discuss "Women's

Votes, Women's Voices." We moved beyond both the "God gap" and the "gender gap" to conclude that women vote, that women have diverse voices, and that women of many faiths share common values with regard to economic and social justice. We demonstrated that virtually all of our groups, from Sikhs and Buddhists to the National Council of Churches, were involved in voter registration. It is this kind of shared commitment, with Christian women *not* in the lead, that shows the necessity and power of diverse religious perspectives.

Future feminist/womanist work has to grapple with the reality of diverse sexualities. As a lesbian feminist, I have been among those who have problematized theologically the matter of sexual orientation or sexual identity, or what I have come to name "sexual integrity," which I think of as the fit between what you see and what you get, what you feel and what you do.[5] With the wonderful Center for Lesbian and Gay Studies in Religion and Ministry thriving at Pacific School of Religion, it may seem rather quaint to suggest that sexual integrity can cause problems. But ask Janie Spahr, an ordained lesbian woman who was prohibited from being called as a minister to a Presbyterian church in Rochester, New York, or Irene Monroe, who is finishing her doctorate at Harvard and writes movingly in the gay press about her experience as an African American religious lesbian, or Beth Stroud, an out lesbian who was recently defrocked by the United Methodist Church in Pennsylvania for her sexual integrity, and it is clear that there is much unfinished business on the lesbian front. In most of the world outside Berkeley, sexuality remains highly problematic.

More than thirty years ago, Sally Miller Gearhart wrote what to my knowledge was the first explicit lesbian feminist theological work. It was a lecture, later an article, titled "A Lesbian Looks at God the Father," which she delivered as part of a pastors' event at Pacific School of Religion in February 1972.[6] The article was rejected for publication by the Program Agency of the United Presbyterian Church but later published by the Philadelphia Task Force on Women in Religion in their pink supplement to their newsletter, *Genesis III*, edited by the noted lesbian activist Nancy Krody. We have long needed, and still need, the space created by women's groups to do our own work.

Sally Gearhart made clear at that time that being a lesbian feminist was different from being a gay man; it was not simply the female equivalent of a gay man because the situation of all women was different from that of all men. And she claimed that same-sex love was connected to other justice struggles and could not be claimed apart from those. Most of the subsequent work in the field of lesbian feminist studies in religion has been in some fashion teasing out the implications of those insights.

Lesbian feminist insights have proceeded in much the same pattern as other feminist work in religion. Pioneering examples include Bernadette Brooten's work on homoerotic relations between women in early Christian communities, Judith Plaskow's insights into Judaism, Carter Heyward's insights into redemption, Virginia Ramey Mollenkott's sensuous spirituality, and my own work on friendship, to mention just a few.[7]

As the seeds took root, several methodological issues emerged in the field. One was the inclusion of heterosexism in the catalogue of kyriarchal oppressions, assuring that many feminist and womanist theologies included this critical lens. Others did not, in large part because it was difficult unto impossible to be identified with even raising this issue and still be taken seriously in many faith communities. Such was and remains the power and price of sexual integrity.

Nonetheless, courageous women, both lesbian/bisexual women and supportive heterosexual women, have spent their intellectual and moral capital in the service of homo-safety by examining the religious dimensions of heterosexism. The work of Traci West and Kelly Brown Douglas stands out in the womanist community.[8] The Pacific Asian and North American Asian Women in Theology and Ministry recently held a consultation here in the Bay Area focused on issues of sexuality, including same-sex love. Kwok Pui Lan has written about the growing gay activism in Asian churches.[9] Lesbian Native American, Buddhist, Muslim, and Hindu colleagues are carrying on the conversation in their circles. More of this will obviously enrich the field.

Two difficult problems make this increasingly complicated. The first is the entrance of transgender persons, whose very being challenges the static binary categories of male/female and by extension lesbian/heterosexual.[10] We used to know who a woman was, what constituted a man. Today, thanks to the patience and perseverance of trans people in communities that don't "get it" easily, none of us can claim to know who is who with the certainty to which we have grown accustomed. However, despite the gender fluidity that has served to destabilize most of our categories, we are clearer than ever about oppression and discrimination. The work ahead is to rethink all of our lesbian/gay/bisexual/transgender/queer analyses in light of this reality and to include and embrace persons and perspectives accordingly. The intellectual challenge is new, but the social/cultural challenge, especially in religious circles, will keep generations busy.

The second problem is that gay/lesbian dynamics in religion have been like gay/lesbian dynamics in the larger arena; namely more gay than lesbian, more white than racially diverse, more Christian than multireligious. While women may even be in the leadership of such efforts, until and unless a specific lesbian feminist/womanist perspective is incorporated, I regret to report that the work remains largely male-focused with all of the attendant power inequality that implies.

The gender inequity is due to the fact that for many, though not all, gay men the primary contradiction is being gay in religious traditions that are hetero-male-dominated, whereas for lesbian women the primary contradiction is being female in traditions that are male-dominated, and the secondary contradiction is being lesbian. This means that women—heterosexual, lesbian, and bisexual—tend to have more in common with one another than do lesbians with gay men, or gay men with heterosexual men. The result is that sexual diversities are more easily incorporated into feminist/womanist work than into the field as a whole. How this dynamic will play out as young people live more easily with gender fluidity remains to be seen. But what is clear is that the backlash against all queer people, especially against queer people of color and against queer Muslims, is dangerous, expensive, and not going away.

These three diversities of identities, religions, and sexualities are part of the contemporary fabric in which any program in feminist/womanist studies in religion in a seminary and university-based institution like the GTU will seek to achieve the goals of equality, justice, and solidarity. Like a three-dimensional tic-tac-toe game, this challenge is far more complicated than what we faced thirty years ago, when I asked Sally Dries where the pool was and what the GTU could offer me as a woman. But so are we far more sophisticated in our analysis, far greater in our numbers, and far richer in our diversity. We have remarkable resources on which to base future work. Because of this, I believe that a program of this sort must have three components:

(1) It must emerge from these many identities, religions, and sexualities, and be structurally connected to the communities of struggle that arise from those diversities, specifically communities of color, queer folks, marginalized women, and their dependent children.

(2) It must have a clearly articulated social change agenda—not simply an intellectual consideration of gender, but a programmatic commitment to creating the conditions for equality using the renewable moral energy of religions.

(3) It must have a global consciousness and reach, together with a critical if humble selfunderstanding of its social location in the superpower that is causing so many of the world's problems. It will, of course, entail an ecofeminist commitment, since protecting the earth is part of the common agenda.

I support such a program wholeheartedly. Some seminaries have shown limited tolerance for innovation and imagination, so the resources of the University of California at Berkeley, and an enlarged role for the Graduate Theological Union as a discrete institution rather than only in the consortium form it currently occupies, are needed. History is the best indicator of what can be done here, and the work of hundreds of women over the decades is proof that much was done with less in the past three decades.

To those who planted the seeds of feminist/womanist theologies, I say, thank you. To those who are nurturing them, I wish courage and perseverance. To those who will see them bloom, I say, share them as widely as you can.

CHAPTER SIX

Muslim Feminism and Islamic Reformation: The Case of Iran

Nayereh Tohidi

SINCE THE INCEPTION OF THE ISLAMIC REPUBLIC IN 1979, gender contestation has gained extra saliency and unprecedented intensity in Iranian society and polity. The current gender regime in Iran and the women's movement challenging it have complex, contradictory, and paradoxical characteristics. To explain one aspect of this complexity concerning Iranian women's negotiation with the ruling patriarchy, I will focus on one of the strategies used by many Muslim reformers, women as well as men, in dealing with the traditional Islamic discourse, particularly the patriarchal construct of Sharia (the Islamic law). As one of the various ways and means of women's struggle, this strategy—known in the West as "Islamic feminism"—represents a resistance and subversion from within the religious framework and Islamic institutions. It is an attempt by Muslim believers to reconcile their faith with modernity and gender egalitarianism.

Though a very important factor, religion is only one determinant of women's status and rights, and its impact is mediated or modified through socioeconomic factors, state policy, the educational system, and other sociocultural institutions.[1] But the recent surge of Islamism ("Islamic fundamentalism") and political instrumentalization of religion has practically increased the significance of the role of Islam, especially the Sharia. Islam, like the other two Abrahamic religions, originated in preindustrial, premodern, and patriarchal social orders. Islamic doctrine has not been peculiarly more sexist than the doctrines of the other two religions. All the three religions have waged battles and wars in the process of coming to terms with modernity, especially with egalitarian changes in gender roles and sexual attitudes. What is rather peculiar about the Islamic world is the lag in the process of secularization and the continuous prominence of religion in politics, especially in the gender and identity politics, which is in part due to socio-economic underdevelopment and a historical legacy of colonialism.

In today's Islamic world, including Iran, three main religious trends have to be distinguished from each other vis-à-vis human and specifically women's rights: conservative traditionalists, liberal reformists (modernists), and radical revolutionary Islamists.

(1) Traditional/conservative Islam: Advocated mainly by traditionalist *ulama* (Muslim clerics) and the traditional layers of popular classes, especially bazaar merchants, this trend insists on preservation of a traditional patriarchal gender regime. They ascribe women to the private domain and consider wifehood and motherhood to be the sole roles and obligations of women. Veiling is used as the main device for the maintenance of strict sex-based division of labor and sex-segregated spaces at both public and private spheres.

To this group, human rights, seen as a secular notion based on an individualistic and human-centered universe, are then incompatible with a God-centered universe that would give primacy to duties (rather than rights) and to the clan/kin/family (rather than the individual). Inequality in male-female rights and duties, as defined in the old Sharia and *fiqh* (Islamic jurisprudence), is justified on the basis of a divine order and natural sex differences.

(2) Liberal/modern or reform Islam: Advocates of this tendency are modern-thinking *ulama*; new Islamic intellectuals, including Islamic feminists who are usually members of the modern educated urban upper and middle classes. The background of this trend goes back to the late nineteenth- and early twentieth-

century modernist Muslim thinkers such as Jamal al-Din Al-Afghani (1838–1897, from Iran), Muhammad Abduh (1849–1905, from Egypt) and the subsequent *jadid* movement in Central Asia.[2] Not much different from their European counterparts of the Enlightenment era, the modernism of this trend has been generally male-centered. Yet, influenced by women's movements and feminist critiques and eager to distance themselves from the conservative traditionalists and Islamists, advocates of reform or modernist/liberal Islam have become increasingly open to and receptive of egalitarian gender relations and feminist ideas. Among the contemporary modernist and progressive Muslim elite in Iran one can see both high ranking clerics such as Ayatollah Hassan Sanei, Hojat ol-Islams Mojtahed Shabestari, Yusefi Eshkevari, and Mohsen Kadivar and lay Islamic intellectuals such as Abdolkarim Soroush, Mostafa Malekian, and Akbar Ganji.

(3) Revolutionary Islamism or radical Islam (neo-patriarchy): Islamism has posed itself as an alternative or solution for all of the social ills and gender-related "moral decadence" experienced in both traditional and modern systems. Its gender agenda, though not always in line with conservative traditionalism, is in reaction to the gender regimes and sexual mores promoted by secular Westernized modernists, liberals, socialists, and feminists. Unlike the very extreme cases of Islamists, such as the Taliban of the extremely underdeveloped and devastated Afghanistan, many are influenced by a more advanced socioeconomic milieu (such as Egypt and Iran) and have been forced to accommodate a gender project that entails some paradoxical implications for women's rights.[3]

This group uses religion as a totalitarian political ideology, as an "ism," hence Islamism, the goal of which is to seize state power, Islamists exploit the sense of alienation and grievances of both women and men of the middle classes and the poor. Unlike traditionalists, by mobilizing women and engaging them in social and political activism, Islamists benefit from the support of many women in their bid for political power. To raise their political competitiveness, and because they are aware of the economic exigencies of the modern urban middle and working classes, especially in terms of the changing role of women, many Islamists accept some role for women in the public sphere as well as the private domain such as women's right to vote and the right to education and employment in many fields. Like the traditionalists, however, they obsessively insist on an "Islamic" dress code (though usually less restrictive than the older traditional code), sex segregation and control of women's sexuality, and a mildly reformed Sharia as the basis of the family law. As a result, many Islamists (as in Iran, Egypt, Turkey, Indonesia, Lebanon, and the like) articulate a neo-patriarchy that may not be as restrictive as the one advocated by the Talibans and Al-Qaeda but is still quite male-supremacist and oppressive.[4]

A clear and fascinating example of the distinctions among these three trends, especially concerning gender and women's rights, can be observed in the current political, theological, and philosophical debates in Iran.[5] Many reformers believe that without the triumph of the modernist *ulama* and intellectuals in their attempts to reform the Sharia and *fiqh*, no democracy and certainly no equal rights for women can be achieved in the Muslim world.

To avoid essentializing Islam, let us cast a glance over some global patterns concerning women's rights and religion within both Islamic and non-Islamic societies as they have inevitably interacted with Islamic politics and gender discourses and the women's movement in Iran.

GLOBAL PATTERNS OF WOMEN'S RIGHTS

The twentieth century has been called "the century of women" because of the significant transformations in women's roles and the increased visibility of women's agency in all social, cultural, and political domains. Thanks to women's movements and feminist intellectual and political interventions, the male-normative understanding and practice of civil and human rights underwent significant egalitarian transformation by the end of the twentieth century. As a number of recent studies reveal, however, a majority of women throughout the world (Muslim and non-Muslim) are still suffering from systemic trends of violence, inequality, discrimination, abuse, and neglect in the home, in the labor market, and in society at large.[6] These trends are especially apparent in situations of international war, civil war, and inter-ethnic conflict; migration and refugee camps; networks of sexual trafficking; "honor killings," dowry-related violence and killing, and genital mutilation; and violence perpetrated or condoned by the state.

Legal changes in favor of equal rights for women and the discourses on women's rights as human rights have yet to be translated into effective policies and practices in many parts of the world, especially in the Muslim world. Many governments in the Muslim world, Islamic and otherwise, refuse to recognize, let alone remedy, discriminatory laws, traditions, and practices that perpetuate the second-class status of women. Sexism is not peculiar to Iran or to the Islamic world; peculiar is the current persistence of patriarchal norms and the strength of resistance to equal rights in many Muslim societies in comparison to the Christian West.

For instance, while the majority of the UN (United Nations) member states, including many Muslim states, have ratified the international bill of rights for women, that is, the Convention on the Elimination of All Forms of Discrimination against Women (CEDAW) adopted by the UN in 1979, many of them have ratified it with reservations, that is, with the right to modify or exclude any of its terms that are not compatible with their domestic/national laws. Actually, more reservations have been attached to CEDAW than to any other convention, some of which are essentially incompatible with the purpose of the treaty—equality of women's rights.[7]

This has resulted in what Ann Elizabeth Mayer has called "the new world hypocrisy": rhetorical strategies that proclaim support for women's equality while pursuing policies that are inimical to women's rights.[8] As Mayer and Jane Bayes and I have documented, this hypocrisy and double-talk about women's rights is not limited to Muslim states. To evade international responsibility with regard to the safeguarding of women's equal rights, the United States invokes its Constitution and the Vatican invokes natural law and church tradition just as Muslim countries invoke Islamic law (Sharia) as incompatible with CEDAW.[9]

Two interesting cases in point are Saudi Arabia and the Islamic Republic of Iran, a brief comparison of which reveals interesting paradoxes about religious patriarchy in modern times. As a result of international pressures and for the sake of public relations and image mending, the patriarchal government of Saudi Arabia has recently joined CEDAW—albeit formally and hypocritically as its numerous Sharia-based reservations indicate. The patriarchal resistance in Iran, however, has succeeded in blocking even a formal and hypocritical ratification of CEDAW. This is a clear evidence that Iranian polity—a hostage in the hands of traditionalist jurisprudence—is still less flexible about Sharia whenever it pertains to women's rights and family law, while in reality women in Iran are far more integrated and visible in public and political domains than women in Saudi Arabia. For example, while Saudi women have been, up to very recently, deprived even of the right to possess individual identity cards and are still deprived of many civil and political rights, including the right to drive cars, Iranian women have achieved more social and political rights than their Saudi counterparts.

Furthermore, Iranian women have been far more politicized from their active and massive participation in social movements since the Constitutional Revolution in 1905–11 up to the 1979 Revolution. Although the 1979 Revolution resulted in an Islamist state and regressive gender policies, it has brought women's issues to the surface, paradoxically speeding up the process of feminist consciousness. Again thanks to a history of revolutionary movements, Iran's polity (as well as its society) is more heterogeneous, diverse, and dynamic than the rather homogeneous and centralized nature of the Saudi state. Therefore, even a diplomatically motivated ratification of CEDAW by the Iranian government can open up a new space for women and reformers both within the parliament and among the opposition to challenge the hypocrisy of the state by pointing to the incompatibility of the present laws, especially the family law and penal code, with the objectives and principles of CEDAW.

Thus, it has been ironically harder to ratify CEDAW in Iran than in Saudi Arabia, as its ratification in Iran has to entail real changes and reforms in the legal system and gender policy of the Islamic regime, while in Saudi Arabia, a hypocritical and formal ratification can be made without much immediate challenge from the society. A growing trend toward secularization, a vigorous debate over democratization, liberal and reform Islam in Iranian society, a higher level of women's social activism, the women's press, feminist consciousness among Iranian women both inside Iran and abroad (among the Iranian diaspora), and the presence of vocal and active Muslim feminists in Parliament (*Majlis*) have all placed the Iranian patriarchy and its main bastion of power, the conservative *shi`a ulama*, in a defensive position.

The Islamic Republic of Iran, therefore, cannot simply and even formally join CEDAW without conceding significant revisions and reformations in its Islamist outlook and patriarchal interpretation of Islam. The reality of the Islamist outlook has rendered the governing traditionalist jurisprudence, the Islamic Sharia, a main barrier against political and legal reforms and democratization, especially in the areas concerning women's equal rights. The gender question has thus become the blind spot of democratization and secularization in Iran.

To untangle this ideological barrier against democracy and equal rights for women, many modernist reformers and democrats have come to believe that a prerequisite for modernity and democratization in the Muslim world in general and in Iran in particular is an Islamic reformation. One recent example that drew international attention is the advocacy of Hashem Aghajari, an Islamic reformer and a university lecturer whose call for "Islamic Protestantism" led to his imprisonment and the death penalty (later reduced to five years of imprisonment thanks to a national and international outcry).

Several other Muslim reformers, including prominent clerics such as Hojat ol-Islams Yusef Eshkevari, Mohammad Mojtahed Shabestari, and Seyyed Muhsen Saeed-zadeh, as well as lay Islamic intellectuals such as Akbar Ganji and Alireza Alavi-tabar, have also called for Islamic reformation, specifically a gender egalitarian interpretation of Islamic texts and the replacement of "traditionalist jurisprudence" (*fiqh-e sunnati*) with "dynamic jurisprudence" (*fiqh-e pouya*). This new reformist trend among Muslim intellectuals, identified in Iran as the "religious intellectuals" (*rowshanfekran-e dini*) or the "new religious thinkers" (*nov andishan-e dini*), represents a modern thinking and behavior that tries to reconcile modernity, democracy, and feminism with Islamic faith. An important dimension of this Islamic reformation is Muslim feminism ("Islamic feminism").

Historically speaking, the extent and degree of the present challenge against the patriarchal and patrimonial relations, especially religious patriarchy in Iran, have been unprecedented. One reason for the present strength and, one hopes, long-term effectiveness of women's challenge to the patriarchal gender regime in Iran has been the recent convergence between faith-based Muslim feminism and secular feminism, exerting pressure against male domination from both within and without a religious framework.

A brief reference again to the politics of ratification of CEDAW by Iran's government may illustrate this further. In December 2001, following a campaign by women's groups and the women's press in Iran (religious as well as secular) that demanded the government join CEDAW, including intense negotiations between the reformist Muslim women deputies and some influential *ulama* in Tehran and Qum in order to earn religious sanction for CEDAW, in Khatami's government proposed draft legislation to the parliament for its ratification, albeit with some reservations attached by the *ulama*.

After an intense deliberation within the cultural commission of the parliament, the legislation was passed. But before being presented to the parliament for final voting at the general assembly, the legislation was placed on hold by the head of the parliament, Hojat ol-Islam Mehdi Karrobi. Since then, women's groups such as the Women's Cultural Center, the women's press such as *Zanan* and *Zanan-e Iran*, and reformist women deputies such as Azam Naseripour (representative of Islamabadgharb) and Shahrbanu Emami (representative of Urumiyyeh) have protested this procedural violation and questioned the reasons behind ending discussion about the CEDAW legislation. Each time, they have been advised to be patient since more urgent matters for deliberation and voting are in order.

In a parliamentary session in early May 2003, when women deputies did not give up and demanded transparent explanation, Karrobi finally admitted that it was because of the intervention and "opposition of the nation's elders (*bozorgan-e qowm*) and the Qum Seminary (*huzeh-ye elmiyyeh Qum*)" that the CEDAW legislation was removed from further discussion. He went on to say that the government was supposed to "consult and resolve some concerns in the minds of our *ulama*" about the incompatibility of CEDAW with Sharia.[10] In response, the online weekly *Zanan-e Iran* has begun collecting a petition for a class action suit against this illegal and procedural violation of parliamentary rules.[11]

The halt in the process of ratifying CEDAW is another indication that the traditionalist Islam along with radical Islamists are still holding an upper hand over the law and legal process concerning gender issues in Iran. This unfortunate reality presents different choices for women of various convictions. While many secular women may see replacement of this religious state with a secular democratic one as the only effective path toward achieving equal rights, for many Islamic women the end of the Islamic state is not necessarily the end of Islamic patriarchy. Unless Islam itself is understood, practiced, and reconstructed in an egalitarian framework, Muslim women cannot feel liberated from sexism and male domination. The project of Islamic feminism, then, is seen by some Iranian Muslim reformers, such as Saeedzadeh and Alavi-tabar, and several non-Iranian Muslim feminists in other Muslim societies as a historical necessity for modernization of Islam and reconciliation of Muslims with new exigencies of changed and changing gender roles and sexuality in modern times.[12]

MUSLIM FEMINISM AND MODERN REFORM IN A GLOBAL CONTEXT

In recent decades many Muslim societies, including the Middle East, have witnessed an unprecedented rise in women's literacy rates (more than 65 percent in 2000 compared to less than 50 percent in 1980 among women age fifteen and older).[13] The traditional gender gap in the realm of education is closing, and in some societies, including Iran, women's enrollment in higher education is becoming equal to or even surpassing men's.

In Iran, in 1976 only 35.6 percent of women were literate. By 1999, the literacy rates rose to 80 percent (the rise for rural women was 17.4 percent to 62.4 percent). As of 2001, 62 percent of students enrolled in Iran's universities are women. This striking advance in women's education has naturally resulted in women's increasing engagement in cultural and social life outside the private realm. Women are not simply the objects of modernity's influence; as a highly educated professional group, they themselves have become significant agents of change and modernization.

But the dramatic increases in literacy rates have not achieved a parallel degree of employment for women in the formal sector of the economy (14.3 percent as of 1999).[14] Changes in the patriarchal and patrimonial structure of the legal system and the political, religious, and economic institutions of Middle Eastern societies in general and Iran in particular—especially family law, family structure, gender stereotypes, and sexual mores—have lagged far behind the modern changes in the levels of socialization and political awareness of the new middle-class women.

In addition to this contradiction in gender dynamics, and in part because of it, women have faced a surge of Islamism and conservatism that has commonly entailed a retrogressive gender agenda. Islamism in the case of Iran, especially during the earlier years of the emergence of the Islamic Republic of Iran, had a blatantly retrogressive impact on women's rights, yet the nature and intensity of that impact have varied among women of different class, ethnic, and religious backgrounds.[15] While Islamism in Iran, as in some other Muslim societies such as Turkey, Egypt, and Malaysia, has brought about many actual or potential setbacks for the individual rights of modernized and privileged urban upper- and middle-class women, and also has furthered sex discrimination against working-class and rural women, it has paradoxically pushed a considerable number of the previously marginalized, recently urbanized middle-class traditional women into social, political, and religious activism.

Islamization of public as well as private life (for instance, head covering of women and girls and sex segregation) has removed certain excuses used by the traditional male authority against entrance of young women and girls into public arenas such as high schools, universities, public transportation, car driving, and the media and movie industries. This development has ironically opened new arenas of intervention for this stratum of women, arenas that were earlier rendered inaccessible to the female Muslim—whether they be physical spaces, including mosques, or intellectual arenas, such as theology debates.

It is against this background and the history of encountering and negotiating with modernity in the Muslim world that during the past two decades a reform-oriented modernist religious feminism—known in the West as "Islamic feminism" or "Muslim feminism"—has grown among Muslim women in societies that are faced with a serious Islamist challenge. This is the gender-related component of a broader reform movement within Islamic thought and Islamic institutions in particular and the larger societies with Muslim majorities in general.

Muslim feminism emerges primarily in cities among some of the highly educated, middle-class professional Muslim women who, unlike many earlier pioneers of women's rights and feminism in the Muslim world who were of secular liberal, socialist ("Western") orientation, are unwilling to break away from their religious orientation and consider Islam a significant component of their ethnic, cultural, or even national identity. An active and illuminating example of this trend is "Sisters in Islam" in Malaysia, whose motto is "Justice, Democracy and Equality."[16]

A growing body of literature on "Islamic feminism" has emerged in the field of Middle Eastern women's studies, stimulating at times useful and at times divisive debates among scholars and activists concerned with women's issues in the Middle East and other Muslim societies, including Iran.[17]

The confusion and controversy begin with the very name "Islamic feminism" and its definition. In the context of Iran, for example, two ideologically and politically opposite groups have expressed the strongest objection to this term and to any mixture of Islam and feminism. On the one hand, the right-wing conservative traditionalists and radical Islamists ("fundamentalists") inside Iran adamantly oppose Islamic feminism because of their strong anti-feminist views and feelings. On the other hand, some expatriate leftist secularist feminists outside Iran hold strong anti-Islamic views and feelings. Both groups essentialize Islam and feminism and see the two as mutually exclusive; hence the term "Islamic feminism" is considered an oxymoron. In the press run by the right-wing hard-liners, feminism or feminist tendencies (*gerayeshha-ye femenisti*) among Muslim sisters have become a subject of attack.

Even Ayatollah Khamenei—the *rahbar* or *vali-ye faqih* (the supreme leader of jurisprudence)—has publicly denounced feminist tendencies during a number of his meetings with women's groups. For example, during a meeting with women deputies of Majlis on October 6, 2001, Khamenei insisted that women should hold only those social positions "that are not contradictory to their innate characteristics and nature." While rejecting any hostility toward women, he warned the deputies against "any feminist tendencies."[18] On the very same day, however, during a panel on "Women Reformers and the Future of the Reform," one of the most outspoken women deputies, Fatima Haqiqatjou, implicitly threatened Islamic authorities about an emerging "dangerous social movement," that is, feminism, should they fail to respond to women's demands.[19]

THE PROBLEM WITH "ISLAMIC FEMINISM"

Aside from the two aforementioned hostile objections to "Islamic feminism" in the Iranian context, in other communities, too, feelings of unease and concern have arisen among some Muslim women activists themselves and also among some scholars and professionals about the confusing and divisive implications that this new categorization—used mainly by secular Western-based feminist scholars—may entail. For example, Omaima Abou-Bakr has raised a number of interesting points about the notion of "Islamic feminism."[20] While not opposing the term as such, she draws our attention to the confusion surrounding the term and its political abuses and offers some useful definitional features from the point of view of a Muslim believer. One main reservation discussed by Abou-Bakr concerns the dynamics of naming and formulating this concept that "says a lot more about the observer, the person who coins, than about the object itself." She warns us about the possible divisive nature of this categorization of Muslim women, as it may imply that if one is not directly dealing with Islamic teaching, the Qur'an, Hadith, and the like, then she is outside the circle of Islamic/Muslim feminists.

One should also bear in mind that in most parts of the world (Muslim and non-Muslim), including Iran, many women's rights advocates, whether religious or secular, do not care or actually refuse to be categorized by any kind of feminist labels. Most women activists, secular or religious, try to do all they can to empower themselves and improve women's rights using a pragmatic approach and an eclectic theoretical framework.

Some Western feminists and journalists have overemphasized Islamic feminism, which may result in two negative repercussions, one political and the other theoretical or conceptual. Politically, this may alarm and further threaten the anti-feminist Islamist patriarchy, causing further reaction against Muslim feminist reformers. Consequently, Muslim women activists may be even more reluctant to associate themselves with feminist discourse in general and secular feminists in particular.

The other potential problem is a sort of Islamic determinism, as an implication of continually "foregrounding the Islamic spirit or influence as the regularly primary force in Middle Eastern societies, hence disregarding the complexities of social/political and economic transformations."[21] In an interview, Shirin Ebadi (a prominent feminist lawyer in Iran) referred to this problematic implication: "If Islamic feminism means that a Muslim woman can also be a feminist and feminism and Islam or Muslimhood does not have to be incompatible, I would agree with it. But if it means that feminism in Muslim societies is somehow peculiar and totally different from feminism in other societies so that it has to be always Islamic, I do not agree with such a concept."[22]

I would also add that to view Islamic feminism as the *only* or the most *authentic* path for emancipation of Muslim women may also imply a sort of orientalistic or essentialist Islamic determinism usually manifested in the views of those who see Islam either as the primary cause of women's subordination or as the only path for women's emancipation. All history up to now, including the case of the Islamic Republic of Iran, has proved both of these approaches wrong. Historically, the interplay of several factors, including geopolitical and socioeconomic developmental forces, colonialism, state policies related to patriarchal culture and religion, and local customs and traditions, has shaped women's status in any given country.

I would also like to draw attention to some practical and conceptual problems associated with the way scholars and activists based in the West name, categorize, and treat the struggles of Muslim women for their human rights, civil rights, and empowerment. It is in the spirit of dialogue, coalition building, inclusiveness, pluralism, and diversity that I would suggest we avoid polarizing a "faith position" and a "secular position" with regard to a commitment to women's rights. To set secular and Islamic feminism in a bitter conflict can only benefit the reactionary patriarchal forces, be it of traditional or new Islamist patriarchy or secular modern patriarchy. To equate secular or modern with equality and feminism is as naïve and misinformed as equating faith and religion with anti-modernity and anti-feminism. Not all Muslims are against equal rights for women, and not all secular people support feminism or women's equal rights.

DEFINITION AND CHARACTERISTICS OF ISLAMIC FEMINISM

Let's make it clear what we mean by Islamic feminism and how we would define it. When it is used as an identity, I personally find the term *Muslim feminist* (a Muslim who is feminist) less troubling and more pertinent to current realties than the term *Islamic feminist*. The latter term seems to be more appropriate as an analytical concept in feminist research and feminist theology or as a discourse. The definition of either term, however, is difficult, since a Muslim feminist (believer) would probably define it differently from a lay social scientist like me. While Christian and Jewish feminisms have a longer and more established place within feminist movements, Muslim feminism as such is a relatively new, still fluid, undefined, more contested, and more politically charged trend. Muslim feminism is one of the ways or discourses created or adopted by certain strata of women (middle-class, urbanized, and educated) in predominantly Muslim societies or in Muslim diaspora communities in response to three interrelated sets of domestic, national, and global pressures of new realities.

Responding to Traditional Patriarchy, Sanctioned and Reinforced by Religious Authorities

While some women activists of the modernized educated upper and middle class see religion, including Islam, as a premodern, oppressive patriarchal institution and maintain a secular or even anti-religious perspective, many others have not broken away from their faith and religious identity. They have tried to resist and fight patriarchy within a religious framework. A basic claim among various religious feminist reformers, including Muslim and Christian feminists, is that their respective religions, if understood and interpreted correctly, do not support the subordination of women. As a theological as well as political response, these reformers maintain that the norms of society and the norms of God are at odds. An egalitarian revision, therefore, is not only possible but also necessary. In reclaiming the "egalitarian past," reformist feminist scholars note that before these religions became closely associated with state power (in the first through fourth centuries of Christianity and in the early years of Islamic tradition in the eighth century), women did hold positions of leadership.

Responding to Modernity, Modernization, and Globalization

As a result of the expanding impact of modernity in Muslim societies (for example, the growing rates of urbanization, literacy, and employment among women as well as men), Muslim women, like women in any modern society, move forward toward egalitarian ideas and feminist reconstruction of modern life, especially of the family structure, gender roles, and gender relations. Muslim feminism is then a negotiation with modernity, accepting modernity (which emerged first in the West) yet presenting an "alternative" that is to look distinct and different from the West, Western modernism, and Western feminism. This is an attempt to "nativize" or legitimize feminist demands in order to avoid being cast as a Western import. As Leila Ahmed argues, "reforms pursued in a native idiom and not in terms of the appropriation of the ways of other cultures" would possibly be more intelligible and persuasive to more traditional classes (and not merely to modern upper and middle classes), and therefore they may prove more durable.[23]

The language and reasoning of reform-minded Islamic women activists in Iran are a clear example of this. The following quotation from Fatima Haqiqatjou, the aforementioned woman deputy in Majlis, represents the way they have been bargaining with patriarchy. During a press conference, she discussed their petition to the president, in which thirty-four deputies had recommended five women candidates for the position of governor of Tehran. But to their disappointment, no women governor was appointed.

> The women fraction of the Majlis has reached a bitter conclusion. Due to a masculinist perspective among the top-level directors and managers, there is a disbelief in women's merits and capabilities for holding managerial positions. . . . We are after improvement of women's status and rights on the basis of religious thinking and ideas and through Iranian and native forms. The Islamic order (*nezam-e Islami*) ought to be able to respond to our aspirations and demands. But if the society and the political will of the state authorities do not allow actualization of women's demands, there will certainly emerge a very dangerous social movement.[24]

Successful or not, this trend is related to the legacy of Western colonialism, a postcolonial insistence on forging and asserting an independent or "native" national identity, including an indigenous or "native feminism," especially in the face of growing globalization. One more aspect of globalization contributing to this trend is the growing transnational migration (which is no longer predominantly a male practice) or the diasporaization or de-territorialization of cultural identities. This has facilitated a wider exposure to global and modern discourses of feminism, human rights, and democracy, which have been directly or indirectly changing women's consciousness and expectations in countries like Iran. The impact of such factors has been intensified through increased access to the Internet, satellite TV, and other communication technology.

Responding to the Recent Surge of Patriarchal Islamism

With the environment growing increasingly Islamist since the 1970s, entailing imposition of a retrogressive gender project, many Muslim women feel compelled to change and improve women's roles and rights within an Islamic framework. For the educated women who want to reconcile the religious dimension of their identity with an empowered social status based on egalitarian gender relationships and freedom of choice in their personal, family, and sociopolitical life, Muslim feminism offers a mechanism to resist and challenge the sexist nature of the ongoing identity politics, particularly Islamism. Some scholars and feminist activists, religious and secular (such as Leila Ahmed, Riffat Hassan, Fatima Mernissi, Shirin Ebadi, and Ziba Mir-Hosseini), see modern liberal and gender egalitarian reformation of Islam as a requirement for the success of a broader societal and political movement toward democracy, pluralism, and civil rights, including women's rights. Such an approach, therefore, would stress the urgent need to equip women with the tools (for instance, knowledge of Arabic, the Qur'an, and *fiqh* as well as feminist knowledge) that enable them to redefine, reinterpret, and reform Islam to be a more women-friendly and gender egalitarian religion. The goal is to enable women to "turn the table" on Islamist authorities, to take Islamist men to task about what they preach and practice in the name of Islam. During a seminar at Radcliffe College, a Muslim feminist put it this way: "The mullahs are trying to use the Qur'an against us, but we have a surprise for them: we're going to beat them at their own game."

In short, I see Muslim feminism or "Islamic feminism" as a spiritual if not a faith-based response of a certain stratum of Muslim women in their negotiation with and struggle against patriarchy (the old traditionalist Islamic patriarchy and the neo-patriarchy of Islamists) on the one hand and the new (modern and postmodern) realities on the other. Its limits and potentials for women's empowerment, however, like those of other ideology-based feminisms, have to be accounted for in its deeds and practices more so than in its theological or theoretical strengths and inconsistencies.

A FEW COMPARATIVE OBSERVATIONS

I would also like to suggest a few comparative and historical observations that may help us with a better feminist strategizing with regard to diversity within the global women's movement as well as the women's movement in Iran vis-à-vis Muslim feminism.

We tend to forget that Islam, like all other religious institutions, is a human or social construct: hence it is neither ahistoric nor monolithic, reified, and static. This becomes more evident when Muslim women's experience is compared to the experience of Christian women.[25] The struggle to reconstruct religion to conform to the new realities of a modern, egalitarian, and democratic gender regime has taken place from both within and without religious institutions, and it has been an ongoing process in the Christian (Protestant and Catholic) contexts.[26] Thanks to the emergence of a stronger middle class, modernity, and a vigorous bourgeois liberal fight for individual rights and humanism, the reformation of religion, secularization, and democratization of society have been achieved much more successfully in the more advanced and industrialized Christian West. In the Muslim context, however, the interplay of geographic and geopolitical disadvantages, colonialism, and underdevelopment has hindered the progress of similar processes, hence further complicating attainment of civil rights, especially women's rights.

Modernist rational and liberal attempts to reinterpret or reform Islam emerged almost a century ago, led by theologians and jurists such as the Egyptian Muhammad Abduh (died in 1905). By the turn of the twentieth century, some Muslim women thinkers and writers had gradually begun framing their gender-conscious and women-friendly writings within Islamic ethics (for example, Tahira Qurratulein, Bibi Khanum Astarabadi, Zeinab Fawwaz, and Ayesha Taymuriya). It is only in retrospect, however, that one may consider them to be Muslim feminists, since such categorization has been formulated very recently and—for the most part—by Western or Western-based feminists and not by Muslim feminists themselves. For instance, when Elizabeth Cady Stanton and her colleagues wrote the *Women's Bible* in 1895, nobody called her a Christian feminist, but today, because of the currency of feminist discourse, Amina Wadud's work in the United States is naturally seen as an example of Islamic/Muslim feminism.[27] Such a naming in the present context can be harmless if it does not imply a deliberate or unwitting "otherizing" or essentializing of Muslim women. It can be harmless if it does not limit the diverse spectrum of women's movements in Muslim societies to Muslim women and to a primarily religious feminism at the expense of ignoring, excluding, or silencing women of non-Muslim religious minorities or women of secular, lay, or atheist orientation.

Like other components of the modern (and arguably postmodern) reform movements within Islam, Muslim feminism too is a Qur'an-centered discourse. The Qur'an, seen as the "eternal and inimitable" text, provides Muslims with both the foundational basis and the point of convergence of many different human interpretations in the light of specific socioeconomic and political situations.[28] Feminist Muslims like Azizah al-Hibri see flexibility and evolution as "an essential part of *Quránic* philosophy, because Islam was revealed for all people and for all times. Consequently, its jurisprudence must be capable of responding to widely diverse needs and problems."[29] Muslims rely on *ijtihad*, which is the ability to analyze a Qur'anic text or a problematic situation within the relevant cultural and historic context and then devise an appropriate interpretation or solution based on a through understanding of Qur'anic principles and the Sunnah.[30]

However, an important challenge for Muslim feminists, some writers such as Anne Sofie Roald argue, is that the Qur'an is seen as the "word of God" and consequently immutable.[31] In response, Muslim modernists (such as Mohammad Mojtahed Shabestari and Abdolkarim Soroush) and feminists have pointed out that the symbolic wording of the Qur'an is not critical.[32] Rather the *interpretation* of the Qur'an by men forms the basis of Islamic law, application, and practice. This male (*ulama*) monopoly of authority to interpret the Qur'an or engage in *ijtihad* is what Muslim feminists are challenging now. Friedl explains this quite clearly in the context of Iran:

> Theoretically these texts are beyond negotiation because they are claimed to emanate from divine or divinely inspired authority. Practically, however, the Holy Writ has to be translated, taught, and made understandable to the faithful, especially to illiterate and semiliterate people who cannot read original Arabic texts. . . . This means it has to be interpreted. Interpretation is a political process: the selection of texts from among a great many that potentially give widely divergent messages, and their exegesis are unavoidably influenced, if not outrightly motivated, by the political programs and interests of those who control the formulation and dissemination of ideologies.[33]

The text is read and understood based on our presuppositions, which vary across time and across cultures, the new Islamic reformers argue. It is with such an approach to religion that the women's press in Iran has embarked on both political and theological debates on gender issues, taking the Islamic reformers (cleric as well as lay) to task through face-to-face encounters, interviews, and panel discussions.

After writing numerous books and articles in the journal *Zanan* (*Women*) of radical and feminist writings based on *ijtihad* in Islamic foundations, Hojat ol-Islam Seyyed Mohsen Saeedzadeh (a young cleric) was imprisoned and after release was defrocked and banned from publishing.[34] Hojat ol-Islam Yusef Eshkevari is another reformist liberal cleric who is still in jail, in part because of his declaration that the *hijab* is not an Islamic mandate.

Similarly, Alireza Alavi-tabar, although a lay scholar, has openly defended feminism, including Islamic feminism, on the basis of clear sociological as well as theological definitions. His progressive ideas and bold, nonsectarian advocacy of women's rights have made him one of the most popular Muslim reformers among Iranian women and men. Alavi-tabar identifies three mechanisms that have been used for reform and reinterpretations of Islamic conjunctions: suspending the primary conjunctions and legislating instead on the basis of the secondary conjunctions and governmental rules; dynamic jurisprudence (*fiqh-e pouya*) of the secondary conjunctions; and *ijtihad* in the Islamic foundations. He argues that although the first two mechanisms are necessary for the articulation of equal rights for women and men, they are not sufficient. As a real solution for the present problem of incompatibility of Islamic *fiqh* with women's equal rights and human rights, and in order to reach truly new and modern perspectives, "advocates of the new religious thinking [*nov andishan-e dini*] have to eventually seek *ijtihad* in the Islamic foundations only."[35] Based on such a radical *ijtihad*, the Islamic jurisprudence (*fiqh*) is seen in its entirety as a secondary (not essential or primary) component of Islam—a human (rather than divine) revelation and historical and time-bound construct, hence subject to change, revision, and reconstruction.[36] When asked what he thinks about the existence or viability of Islamic feminism, Alavi-tabar responded:

> It depends on what we mean and how we use this concept. If it means that one can advocate equal social and legal rights for women and men while remaining loyal to religious ethics and values, it is certainly

present here and viable too. Islamic feminism is a call for re-reading of our interpretations of the Islamic texts and history of religious life. By putting aside the patriarchally-inspired values and tendencies, and upholding a new perspective, many of what have been taken for granted as "obvious sharià" ought to be questioned and proved that they are not obvious elements of sharià, but products of our worldly way of livings and traditions. . . . Islamic feminism, in this sense, is very close to the project of modern religious intellectualism.[37]

Like other modernist reform movements within religion, Muslim feminism emphasizes individual agency and insists upon women's right to a direct relationship with God with no human (cleric) mediators. Based on the idea of intersubjectivity, this makes the individual (female or male) and God the subjects of interaction rather than the male cleric and the female or male believer. Such intersubjectivity has been a basic principle of reformation within Christianity since it was promoted by Martin Luther in 1551.[38] This principle, if applied seriously among Muslims, can challenge the (male) clerical monopoly over religion, transforming women's understanding of religion from a male cleric–centered authoritarian institution to a nonhierarchical spiritual entity, involving both individual and group-based processes in women's daily lives.

POLICY IMPLICATIONS: PERILS AND PROMISES

Feminist believers from the three Abrahamic religions (Judaism, Christianity, and Islam) have a lot to learn from each other's experience in "reclaiming" their faith and spirituality from the clergy-centered patriarchal monopoly of religious authorities. Achievement of women's rights in Iran or any other Muslim society cannot depend solely or even primarily on women's reinterpretation of Islamic texts. Since a literal reading of the Qur'an, like other scriptures, is male supremacist, and most Muslims and non-Muslims are still more inclined to accept male authority without question, more should be done to reeducate men at home and in school.

But spiritual feminism and faith-based feminists, including Islamic feminists, will not be much different from religious fundamentalists if they do not respect the freedom of choice and diversity and if they try to impose their version of feminism on secular, lay, and atheist feminists. What can be troubling in regard to religious feminism, be it Islamic or Christian, is the tendency toward sectarianism or totalitarianism. The real danger is when a single brand of ideological feminism, be it secular Marxist or religious Islamic (in this case it becomes Islamist), presents itself as the only legitimate or authentic voice for *all* women or the "true path for liberation," negating, excluding, and silencing other voices and ideas among women in any given society. Appreciation for ideological, cultural, racial, sexual, and class diversity is critical for local and global feminist movements.

For effective feminist strategizing, the importance of dialogue, conversation, and coalition building among women activists of various ideological inclinations cannot be overemphasized. The feminist movement is not one movement but many. What unites feminists is a belief in human dignity, human rights, freedom of choice, and further empowerment of women rather than any ideological, spiritual, or religious stance. Secularity works better for all when secularism means impartiality toward religion, not anti-religionism.

Some secularist and Marxist feminists have treated Muslim or Christian feminists as rivals or foes of secular feminism and have been preoccupied with academic concerns over their philosophical and ideological inconsistency and postmodern limits (as though various brands of secular feminism are free from such limits). We may see religious and spiritual feminism, including Muslim feminism, as a welcome addition to the wide spectrum of feminist discourse, as long as these religious feminists contribute to the empowerment of women, tolerance, and cultural pluralism. When their discourse and actions impose their religious strictures on all, however, when they co-opt the meaning of feminism to fight against equal rights for women or women's empowerment, or when they cooperate with and serve as arms of repressive and anti-democratic Islamist states, Muslim feminism is not helpful. Muslim feminism serves women's cause when it complements, diversifies, and strengthens the material as well as spiritual force of women's movements in any given Muslim society.

Observations of the recent Islamist and other religious fundamentalist movements indicate that theocratic states are not able to empower women or to provide an inclusive democracy for their citizens. Religion is important but should be separated from state power. Muslim feminists seem to be an inevitable and positive component of the ongoing change, reform, and development of Muslim societies as they face modernity. In the short run, Muslim feminists may serve as a sort of Islamization of feminism for some. In the long run, in a society that allows for and protects open debate and discussion, Muslim feminism (as Christian feminism did) can facilitate the modernization and secularization of Islamic societies and states. Negotiating modernity takes many forms. Although feminism and women's movements have become more global than ever before, as a Jewish feminist colleague, Simona Sharoni, once noted, sisterhood is not global, nor is it local; women's solidarity has to be negotiated within each specific context.

Women's experiences in many Muslim and non-Muslim societies show that women's rights and empowerment and democratization in general cannot be left wholly in the hands of the elites (female or male) and their theological and intellectual debates but rather must be pushed and supervised by elements from broader civil society and women's grassroots movements and organizations. Though important, Muslim/Islamic reformism and feminism are only one necessary component of social transformation toward women's equal human rights. Economic changes that provide women with equal opportunities for gainful employment, changes in gender-based division of labor, integration of women into political processes and decision making, and egalitarian shifts in cultural stereotypes about gender roles and gender relations and double standards in sexual mores are all necessary processes of improvements in women's status in Iran and other parts of the Muslim world.

MODERNITY AND WOMEN IN THE MUSLIM WORLD

Historically speaking, sexism has not been peculiar to Islam or the Islamic world. What is peculiar is that a visible gap has emerged in modern times between the Islamic world and the Christian West with regard to the degree of egalitarian improvement in women's rights. This gap has been due to the legacy of colonialism, underdevelopment, defective modernization, the weakness of a modern middle class, democratic deficit, the persistence of cultural and religious patriarchal constructs such as Sharia as a result of the failure of reform and secularization within Islam, and weakness of civil society organizations—especially women's organizations—in the Muslim world.

The recent surge in identity politics, Islamism, and religio-nationalist movements is in part the outcome of socioeconomic and cultural dislocation as well as polarization and alienation caused by modernization, Westernization, and globalization. It is also a "patriarchal protest movement" in reaction to the challenges that the emergence of modern middle-class women poses to traditional patriarchal gender relations. The main premise of this article is that the processes of democratization, civil society building, and consolidation of civil rights and universal human/women's rights are intertwined with reformation in Islam, feminist discourse, and women's movements.

Gender has become the blind spot of democratization in the Islamic world. In terms of national and international policy implications, it should be recognized that women and youth have become the main forces of modernization and democratization in the Islamic world, especially in Iran. Democracy cannot be consolidated without a new generation of Muslim leaders and state elites who are more aware of the realities of a globalized world and more committed to universal women's and human rights.

To win the war against terrorism and patriarchal Islamism, we need more than military might. In the short and medium term, a just resolution of the Israeli-Palestinian conflict can alter the present social-psychological milieu that has allowed the growth of extremism and male-biased identity politics. In the long term, democratization and comprehensive gender-sensitive socio-economic development seem to be the only effective strategies. A significant component has to be Islamic reformation, which requires international dialogue with and support for secular as well as religious egalitarian and democratic voices in the Muslim world.

CHAPTER SEVEN

Appreciating the Lineage
of Buddhist Feminist Scholars

Sandy Boucher

THE COMING OF BUDDHISM FROM ASIA TO THE WEST constitutes one of the most complex and exciting phenomena in the annals of world religion. In the roughly forty years since its introduction in the United States, Buddhism has met with and incorporated various distinctly Western elements, most dramatically the full participation of women, the fruit of what Rita Gross famously called "the auspicious meeting of Buddhism with Feminism."

Those of us who have practiced, studied, written, and organized in the midst of this always challenging, sometimes contentious relationship have benefited tremendously from the work of Buddhist women scholars. These thinkers have helped us envision the inclusion of women's priorities and awareness even when that consciousness did not exist in the practice settings in which we found ourselves. They helped us balance the revelations engendered by our newfound spiritual practice with the fact that as women we have sometimes been denied or dismissed in our Buddhist institutions and in the traditional texts.

My own story begins around 1981. I had been doing Buddhist meditation practice with Ruth Denison in the Mojave Desert. A European-born woman who received authorization to teach in the lineage of Burmese master U Ba Khin, Ruth teaches mindfulness by strongly incorporating awareness of the body. She uses movement and dance (as well as traditional sitting and walking meditation) to deepen our insight, and she brings attention to our interdependence with all phenomena. I was challenged and richly rewarded by this practice. And I found myself curious about the larger world of Buddhist teachings, history, and institutions, particularly the role of women in Buddhism.

On the lookout for information, I happened upon two works by British women that opened the door to my own awareness of participation in what I would call a "lineage" of Buddhist-feminist scholars. In Buddhism the concept of lineage has traditionally been honored: after exceptional effort and achievement, one could be invited to take one's place in a line of practitioners extending back to Shakyamuni Buddha himself. And while this concept of lineage has proven problematical in some Western settings, I wholeheartedly take my place in the line of women scholars that began with Caroline Rhys Davids.

The book she translated and edited, which was published in 1909, is called *The Psalms of the Early Buddhists, Vol. I: Psalms of the Sisters*, or, in its original Pali, *The Therigatha*.[1] It presents and comments upon the enlightenment verses composed by the "sisters," the nuns who lived and achieved liberation during the Buddha's lifetime in fifth-century BCE India and for several centuries afterwards. This volume of verses and commentary contains the stories of women in ancient India who had struggled against the cruelly restrictive conditions of their lives in order to be able to "go forth into the homeless life" of the spiritual seeker in the brown robes worn by the Buddha. Here in Rhys Davids's book I found women's voices telling of their suffering and exulting in their awakening from that suffering through the very practice that I was doing in twentieth-century America.

For instance, a woman named Mutta sings:

O free, indeed! O gloriously free
Am I in freedom from three crooked things:—
From quern [mill for grinding grain], from mortar,
    from my crookback'd lord!
Ay, but I'm free from rebirth and from death,
And all that dragged me back is hurled away. [2]

Or Mitta, who talks about the satisfactions of the monastic life:

To-day one meal, head shaved, a yellow robe—
Enough for me. I want no heaven of gods.
Heart's pain, heart's pining, have I trained away. [3]

I found this collection of verses and commentary tremendously affecting. To reach back twenty-five hundred years into the religious experiences of these women left me feeling that I had touched some actual, almost physical grounding in a female understanding of the Buddha's teachings. This inspired me and strengthened my own resolve to pursue this practice. Women had done it. Women had achieved full liberation and were named in the canon, their stories told, their accomplishments extolled. And all this had happened in ancient India. How much more possible ought it to be to move forward in the practice in my much less repressive world of 1980s North America. In this volume I also discovered female teaching lineages among those early women practitioners, many of whom went to female teachers for their training and acknowledgment of their spiritual progress. And this discovery validated my own choice to practice with a teacher of my own sex.

Learning more about the translator of *Psalms of the Sisters*, I found that Caroline Rhys Davids is almost universally referred to as "Mrs. Rhys Davids" in the hundreds of citations of her work, a locution from a time when marital status signaled a certain respectability. A clue to her identity as a feminist leapt out at me when I opened *Psalms of the Sisters*: the dedication— "To Olive Schreiner, seer of 'dreams.'" This homage to Schreiner, the South African novelist and feminist, places Rhys Davids firmly in the stream of the early women's movement. *Psalms of the Sisters* was published in 1909, nine years before the women of Rhys Davids's native Britain won the right to vote. She was sensitized and seasoned by that fifty-year struggle for equality into an enhanced awareness of women's conditions and compromised status. She was supported in her own scholarly efforts by her participation in a movement and her connection with other activist women.

Rhys Davids held a distinguished position in the world of Buddhist scholarship in England, where she was a major Pali-language scholar and translator, often working with her husband, T. W. Rhys Davids, founder of the Pali Text Society; she was a fellow of University College, London; and she served as president of the Pali Text Society for twenty years, until her death in 1942. The Pali Text Society was and is engaged in translating the books of the Pali canon into English.[4] Rhys Davids's academic work in Indian philosophy and the history of Buddhism, as well as her many translations, contributed substantially to this effort. She mothered three children, one of them a son who became a pilot in the First World War and was killed in action. She was an alpine mountaineer. She did charitable work for women and children, and she was not just a sympathizer but a campaigner for women's suffrage.

This life of a woman born in 1857 may sound familiar to many women who give themselves to academic and other work, family, and political-social activism, balancing the demands of these disparate realms as best they can. It was immensely encouraging to me to discover, once again, that contributions are almost never made from an isolated or individualistic position, that Caroline Rhys Davids, as a woman thinker, writer, and teacher, learned from her sisters and could depend upon the support of their shared perspective and struggle to sustain her.

The next link in the chain emerged for me in the work of I. B. Horner, another British scholar born four decades after Rhys Davids. It came as no surprise that she had mentored Horner. In a used bookstore I located Horner's volume, published in 1930, titled *Women under Primitive Buddhism*. When I opened the book, I found this beginning to the prefatory note: "The subject of this book was proposed to me by Mrs. Rhys Davids. I should like to express my deep gratitude to her for her invaluable suggestions, criticism and help, and for her constant interest throughout the progress of this work."[5]

Women under Primitive Buddhism presents a complex portrait of the lives of Indian women twenty-five hundred years ago. First Horner analyzes the societal roles open to these women—mother, daughter, wife, widow, worker—creating a rich sociocultural context for the section that follows, which elucidates the spiritual experiences and opportunities of women who chose to take the robes and become almswomen or remained deeply committed laywomen. Scholarly in tone and amply footnoted, the book allowed me to see how women's spiritual path in Buddhism grew out of the secular and religious life of ancient India. It fed my hunger for information on the ancient roots of the practice in which I participate. Horner opened a world to me, one that informed my thinking and offered a model for my own exploration in writing about the phenomenon of American women's participation in Buddhist practice.

I. B. or Isaline Blew Horner was born in 1896. After earning her degree at Newnham College, Cambridge, Horner traveled in Asia, where she became interested in Buddhism. She returned to Newnham College to serve as a fellow and librarian, and she began her extensive efforts as translator of Pali texts. On Rhys Davids's death, Horner took up the older woman's duties, stepping in to act for seventeen years as honorary secretary of the Pali Text Society; and then from 1959 until her death in 1981, Horner served as president and honorary treasurer of the society. She was very active in mentoring women scholars throughout her career.

It is demurely noted in the short biography provided by the University of Cambridge, where her papers are housed, that "she lived with her companion Elsie Butler [from] 1926 [to] 1959." While this clue could mean more than one thing, I am told by Professor Grace Burford, who is in the process of writing a book-length biography of Horner, that Elsie Butler was what we would now call Horner's "partner," meaning that I. B. Horner was a lesbian living in a long-term committed relationship with another female scholar at the college. This footnote to her life may or may not illuminate her commitment to women in her work, but as a lesbian I was intrigued to note this relationship that might otherwise have remained hidden.

Rhys Davids wrote the preface to *Women under Primitive Buddhism*, praising Horner for presenting "a coherent living picture of the life in the world of the woman, who saw the inception of the New Word, now known as Buddhism." Rhys Davids pointed out that the liberation offered by this new spiritual path meant "the expansion of [woman's] essential nature as human being apart from her femininity." Modern Buddhist women might be suspicious of such a formulation because it denies the importance of the concerns and perspectives that female nature brings into women's practice situations as a component of their spiritual path. But Horner has evoked a time and society in which one's feminine gender alone prescribed a life of severe limitation and subservience, helping readers understand that the ancient Indian woman seeker might want to separate what she saw as her "essential nature" from this burdensome "femininity" and take on a gender-neutral role.

Most powerfully, Horner's book gives the enormous gift of acknowledging the multiplicity of conditions and influences on the spiritual lives of these women. We see them through the prism of their society and their historical period, reminding us that no matter how liberating or transcendent our spiritual attainments, they occur in the actual material/social/economic/political/intellectual world we inhabit and are to whatever extent shaped by these. Or, as her mentor Rhys Davids says, "Especially do I commend her treatment of woman's life, there and during that time, as a whole, and not merely that life as given to 'religion.' The latter loses balance and proportion if considered apart from the former."

As feminist Buddhists we engage the challenge of balancing the realities of our lives in the world with the boundless freedom of our deepest spiritual awareness.[6] Horner's women in ancient India were doing the same thing. It is significant that for many of those early Indian women, the actual moment of enlightenment came in the midst of domestic duties—emptiness piercing through the forms available to women at that time in the only labors allowed them.

So we hear that a woman named Little Sturdy achieved enlightenment when she burnt the dinner over the cooking fire and realized the truth of impermanence. And a follower of Patacara, a woman teacher, tells of finding freedom from the unbearable grief of losing a child.

Lo! from my heart the hidden shaft is gone,
The shaft that nestled there she hath removed,
And that consuming grief for my dead child
Which poisoned all the life of me is dead.
Today my heart is healed, my yearning stayed.[7]

In 1979, almost fifty years after Horner's book appeared, an American woman scholar took up the pen to give us *Women in Buddhism: Images of the Feminine in Mahayana Tradition.*[8] Diana Paul, then an assistant professor of religious studies at Stanford University, was inspired by the work of Catholic theologian Mary Daly to explore a different Buddhist tradition than had Rhys Davids and Horner. She looked at the texts of Mahayana Buddhism (which includes Zen, Pure Land, and other North Asian forms), in which she found misogyny as well as stories of defiant mythical women or female deities in revolt against the idea, for instance, that to attain full enlightenment, a woman had to be reborn as a man. Paul analyzes verses very different from the exultant songs of *The Therigatha*. Verses such as the following were designed to demonize women in order to protect male monastics from temptation.

Ornaments on women
Show off their beauty.
But within them there is great evil
As in the body there is air.

The dead snake and dog
Are detestable,
But women are even more
Detestable than they are.[9]

Women in Buddhism brilliantly explores the textual antecedents and atmosphere that determined the view and treatment of women in Mahayana Buddhist religious settings. Interestingly, Paul's book contains a preface by I. B. Horner.

Next came Tsultrim Allione's *Women of Wisdom*.[10] Published in 1983, this study was developed from Allione's master's thesis and takes us into Vajrayana Buddhism or Tibetan Buddhism. *Women of Wisdom* presents the biographies of six Tibetan female mystics. It is preceded by an introduction describing Allione's personal journey from her young adult years as a Tibetan Buddhist nun in Asia to her disrobing and starting a secular life in the United States, continuing her strong Buddhist practice through two marriages and the raising of three children. This autobiographical introduction gives us a modern-day hero's voyage of sorts within Buddhism, parallel to the heroic lives of the Tibetan female mystics presented in the body of the book.

At this time, through my own practice and study, I began to long for an overview of American women's participation in Buddhist practice. How did they deal with experiences such as working with or becoming teachers, living in community, instances of sexual power abuse by Buddhist teachers, the balancing of child care and practice, monasticism and social activism? I had read Rick Fields's *How the Swans Came to the Lake*,[11] an otherwise excellent history of Buddhism in the United States that only very peripherally mentions women. I thought it likely that if the actual women practicing, teaching, and innovating American Buddhism in the early 1980s were not documented, they would sink away into oblivion, and the male history of Buddhism in America would continue to seem to be the only history. So I set out on a pilgrimage, staying in Buddhist centers and people's spare rooms, talking to a hundred women— students, teachers, mothers, scholars, nuns, lesbians, people long steeped in Buddhist practice, and some just new to the Dharma. I listened to, taped, and photographed each woman, then went on to the next. My bag of audiotapes, notes, and rolls of film grew so heavy that my arms hurt from carrying it as I took planes, trains, and buses all over the country. In this process the major issues engaging Buddhist women were identified and clarified. The resultant book, *Turning the Wheel: American Women Creating the New Buddhism* (first published in 1988, reprinted in 1993),[12] became a compendium of women's voices exploring a spiritual path and confronting the difficulties created by male supremacist thinking and institutions, as well as celebrating the liberating effects of our Buddhist practice.

I wonder if a similar urgency motivated the numerous Buddhist women scholars who have published books since then. Imagine a woman, a hundred years or five hundred years in the future, as she enters Buddhist practice. If she wants to understand women's participation in and contribution to her chosen spiritual path, she will find books in which our voices speak to her of our experiences. As a Buddhist woman, she stands deep in time, connected back over two millennia to the female elders who composed the verses in *The Therigatha* but also to North American women grappling with the issues that arose in the early years of Buddhism's presence on our shores.

Karma Lekse Tsomo, an American woman who is a nun in the Tibetan Buddhist tradition, holds a PhD and teaches at the University of San Diego. She chronicles the lives, struggles, and teachings of female Buddhist monastics in books such as her 1988 *Sakyadhita: Daughters of the Buddha*.[13]

Rita Gross, of the University of Wisconsin, Eau Claire, has been an insightful commentator on the conjunction of Buddhism with feminism for decades, her work culminating in the 1993 publication of *Buddhism after Patriarchy: A Feminist History, Analysis and Reconstruction of Buddhism*.[14] This visionary book provides a capsulation and clarification of the thinking of Buddhist feminists in the preceding decade and offers a feminist revalorization of Buddhism—that is, it does the "work of repairing the tradition . . . bringing it much more in line with its own fundamental values and vision than was its patriarchal form." Epitomizing the development of our perspective since the time of Rhys Davids and Horner, Gross urges a rejection of androcentric and gender-neutral approaches in favor of a Buddhist androgynous reconceptualization. She offers a vision of a Western Buddhism stripped of its misogynist elements, fully incorporating the experience and needs of women, a vision possible to achieve in our twenty-first-century Western practice.

Miranda Shaw, assistant professor at the University of Richmond, became convinced through her research into ancient Tantric (esoteric) texts that women had participated in and attained mastery in all areas of Tantric Buddhism. She published *Passionate Enlightenment: Women in Tantric Buddhism*[15] in 1994 to put forth this theory, igniting controversy among scholars who found it difficult to entertain the possibility that some of the earliest Tantric masters may have been women. In 1995 Anne Klein, an associate professor at Rice University, wrote *Meeting the Great Bliss Queen: Buddhists, Feminists, and the Art of the Self*.[16] Klein's book explores questions of selfhood in feminist and Buddhist theory.

Latest in the explorations of the feminine in Buddhism is Judith Simmer-Brown's 2001 book, *Dakini's Warm Breath: The Feminine Principle in Tibetan Buddhism*.[17] Brown, who is professor and chair of the religious studies department at Naropa University, investigates the role of the *dakini*, a feminine figure who represents the inner wisdom-mind of the practitioner and who often arrives to bestow crucial insight upon a seeker.

This lineage of women scholars (which includes many more I might have named) forms a dynamic continuity and community with the women meditating in Buddhist centers, with the female Buddhist teachers who have made their way often against considerable odds in male-dominated environments, and with the Buddhist men who recognize feminist issues in their religious settings and support the equality of women there.

In 1981 I could find exactly two books about women in Buddhism. Now, twenty-five years later, there are numerous volumes written by scholars and practitioners who have looked deeply into our particular female experience of Buddhist practice and institutions. Ours is a vital, rich lineage integral to the creation of a uniquely American form of Buddhism. Twenty-five years after I found *The Therigatha*, I still receive each new Buddhist feminist book with enthusiasm and gratitude.

The role of women's studies in religion programs in encouraging and supporting this progress has been crucial. My own experience with the Center for Women and Religion at the Graduate Theological Union may illustrate this dynamic influence. From 1988 to 1990 I was studying for a master's degree in the history and phenomenology of religion, affiliated with Starr King School for the Ministry. Another and equally important affiliation was with the Center for Women and Religion. I attended meetings at the little CWR house tucked in next to a parking lot. In its comfortable living room I ate at many potlucks, helped organize events, and taught a class on women and Buddhism.

Then in 1995 some of us from CWR came together to create a delegation to the United Nations Fourth World Conference on Women in Beijing. For months beforehand we met regularly to shape a workshop that we could take to the Beijing conference that would allow for an experience of women's spirituality without imposing any particular creed or perspective and without requiring the participants to be fluent in English. As far as I know, we were the only group offering a workshop to address spiritual issues at this secular world gathering. At our extremely well-attended workshop, women from every part of the world gathered under shields we had created bearing symbols such as a tree, a lotus blossom, a cup, a bird in flight. Participants told their stories of spiritual sustenance, then drew and painted some representation of them on giant sheets of paper hung on the walls, creating a mural. We closed with a spiral dance led by a Native American woman who drew us into a circle of shared spirituality. Participants thanked us for the opportunity to share their spirituality with women from other cultures and creeds in that gathering of activist women from throughout the world.

Without the Center for Women and Religion to support us, we never would have been able to plan and present that workshop, because it grew from the woman-consciousness explored, cultivated, embodied, and expressed by CWR members over the years and strongly held by the institution itself.

Women now attending seminaries desperately need the instruction and support offered by women's studies in religion: to explore women's traditions and develop perspectives on their particular female path and contributions. Voices can speak across generations. When we discover that others have dealt with difficulties like ours, faced challenges, and achieved insight, a light is shone into the dark corners of our own experiences. No one needs to feel isolated or discouraged if she knows her true history. And we need to hear the voices of women from all religious traditions, ethnic groups, sexual persuasions, and economic levels.

As a Buddhist woman, I feel a particular urgency that "Women and Buddhism," "Feminism and Buddhism," and other such courses be included in any women's studies in religion curriculum. As a major religion involving many hundreds of millions of the world's population,

Buddhism deserves to be studied and explored. Many practitioners in the Christian and Jewish traditions have found Buddhist meditation practices helpful in accessing deeper levels of insight within their own faith traditions, while scholars for years have been deepening the Buddhist-Christian dialogue, strengthening the ties between the two traditions. In California this inclusion is even more natural, for we sit on the Pacific Rim; here on the West Coast we look not to Europe or the Middle East but to Asia. Our far western population includes substantial numbers of Asian-born people. Our aesthetics, our cuisine, our philosophy and spirituality—all are generously influenced by Asian culture and thought. Buddhism as one manifestation of that influence deserves to be included in any program on religion. And the resultant conversation among women of different faiths may help us find common ground to heal the tragic split between the transcendent, compassionate core teachings of all religions and the violent conflicts among religious adherents that currently afflict our world.

CHAPTER EIGHT

Women, Religion, and the Challenge of the Ecological Crisis

Mary Evelyn Tucker

MAGNITUDE OF THE ECOLOGICAL CRISIS

The global ecological crisis with all of its local manifestations is a challenge that supercedes all others at the moment. If the global ecosystems and climate are so severely compromised by human action, we will join the list of endangered species. This ecological crisis, then, is the ultimate challenge for religion, for spirituality, for ethics, for theology. This is a historic moment that we are facing, unprecedented in human history. What kind of response can the world's religions give to this issue? What kind of hope can we as women, can we as people of faith, offer to this situation? Because it is very clear, from all the assessments, that humans are destroying the matrix of life on the planet by our overextended presence and aggressive technologies. It is as simple and as complex as that.

Many people are aware, for example, of the reports that Earth's climate is deteriorating with greenhouse gas emissions. They realize that global warming means that the icecaps are melting, hurricanes are increasing, and ocean flooding will affect millions of people living in coastal areas and on islands. Indeed, the future of small island nations in the Pacific are at risk, and they are suing the United States for our reckless involvement with exacerbated climate change.

A report issued in March 2005, the *Millennium Ecosystem Assessment*, is a dire warning to humanity.[1] This report was the result of four years of work; thirteen hundred scientists contributed to it; ninety-five countries participated in the study; and it was supported by the United Nations Fund, the Packard Fund, the United Nations Environment Programme, and other funders.

This is the most comprehensive survey of the state of the planet ever undertaken. It concludes definitively that human activities threaten Earth's ability to sustain future generations. The way society obtains its resources has caused irreversible changes that are degrading the natural processes that support all life on Earth. Jonathan Lash, director of the World Resources Institute, warns that the *Assessment* is essentially an audit of nature's economy and the audit shows we have driven most of the accounts into the red.

The *Assessment* shows that humans have changed Earth's ecosystems beyond recognition in a dramatically short space of time. The assessment observes that the various ways society has obtained its food, fish, fresh water, timber, minerals, fiber, and fuel over the past fifty years have seriously degraded the global environment. Moreover, the current state of affairs is likely to be a roadblock to the Millennium Development Goals (MDG) agreed to by world leaders at the United Nations in 2000—reducing poverty, hunger, disease, illiteracy, discrimination against women, and environmental deterioration by 2015, all of these key issues for women around the world.

When we look at the instruments of change affecting ecosystems, we see that across the board they are increasing in severity: namely climate change, habitat disruption, invasive species, overexploitation of resources, and pollution. All of this deleterious human-based activity underscores the fact that we are now causing a sixth extinction period. The other five extinction periods were induced by external changes such as asteroids or climate change. We are now tipping this tide of destruction. This means that 10 to 30 percent or more of mammals, fish, and amphibians are now becoming extinct. This has tremendous implications for all life forms. This is effecting the depletion of fisheries around the world, including both of our North American coasts. It means that the great apes and many other mammals most likely will not survive in the wild. A scientific project is being initiated to save amphibians, which are declining significantly.

One of the co-conveners of this ecosystem assessment, Angela Crocker, notes that the range of current responses is not commensurate with the nature, the extent, or the urgency of the situation that is at hand. We are losing ground. Does this leave us sleepless? I think it should.

What, then, is the response of the religious communities to this massive loss of life? The fact that humans are causing these extinctions is something to which we, as women and men of faith who are committed to the flourishing of life, need to respond. The environmental crisis is an issue of primary importance for each of the world's religions. As many have recognized, this crisis is, in a fundamental way, an ethical and spiritual issue.

Fortunately, a growing body of scholarly literature and theology as well as grassroots projects are emerging from the world's religions. Ecotheologians and ecofeminists have been leading the way in this regard. Liberation theologians such as Leonardo Boff are now including both the human and the more-than-human world in their reflections. Harvard University's project on world religions and ecology is an important step in this direction, as is the Alliance for Religion and Conservation in England.

In addition to the response of each of the world's religions, interreligious dialogue is absolutely essential. It is necessary to increase tolerance and understanding by discussing the nature of God or the development of human ethics from different perspectives and to move toward transcending our differences—giving us a sense of common identity with the planet, with all species, and with all generations, past and future. This larger type of cosmological, Earth, and species identity is what we need as a grounding for effective interreligious dialogue on the environment and on social-political-economic change.

Some of this movement toward a broader planetary identity is already under way. The conferences on world religions and ecology that my husband, John Grim, and I directed helped to establish the foundations for the world's religions to contribute to this large embrace of planet and people. Area specialists in different religions, including Rosemary Ruether, helped to shape the conferences and edit the ten volumes that resulted. Some eight hundred scholars, theologians, historians of religion, environmentalists, and activists participated in the conferences. Together they began to identify some of the remarkable ecological resources that we have in these traditions: spiritual, ritual, ethical, scriptural. In organizing the conferences, producing the volumes, supporting a journal, and creating a Web site on world religions and ecology, under the Harvard University Center for the Environment, a new field of study is emerging.[2] This field has important implications for environmental studies within the academy and for environmental policies beyond the academy. This work is far from finished. It needs broad participation from the world's religious leaders and laity, more effective leadership, and widespread grassroots activism. It also requires the scholarly theological community to be more involved, along with committed people of faith.

Some of the key leaders in this movement have already begun to emerge. From within the Buddhist tradition, the Dalai Lama and Thich Nhat Hahn have been speaking on the need for environmental protection for several decades. Moreover, for the last eight years, the patriarch of the Greek Orthodox Church, Bartholomew, has led symposia on the environmental crises of the seas. A Greek laywoman, Maria Beckett, has played a key role in constructing those symposia, which have brought together leaders from the United Nations and the European Union, along with scientists, journalists, politicians, and religious leaders. The symposia focused on the state of the seas, which are dying from pollution, overnutrification, and overfishing.

Moreover, Rowan Williams, the archbishop of Canterbury, has issued a major statement that the Anglican Church in England and throughout the world needs to move forward on environmental issues. A number of key women are working in the United Kingdom on this, including

Mary Grey, Anne Primavasi, Celia Drummond, and other theologians. Women theologians in Asia, such as Chung Hyun Kyung, and in Latin America, such as Ivone Gebara, are helping to activate the churches.

Nayereh Tohidi, a Muslim scholar, knows that one of the most interesting ecological movements in the Islamic world is taking place in Iran. In June 2001 and again in May 2005, the Iranian government in cooperation with the United Nations Environment Programme (UNEP) organized conferences in Tehran. A key leader of this movement is the vice president of Iran and the head of their environment ministry, Dr. Massoumeh Ebtekar. She is helping to illustrate that the tenets of Islam are crucial to the survival of the Middle East. In Tehran, ensuring a supply of clean water for twelve million people is clearly a critical issue, as it is throughout the Middle East. Leadership is emerging in very interesting areas, sometimes behind the scenes but often with women centrally involved.

Both leadership on a high government level and grassroots activism of women around the world have been essential to this movement of religion and ecology. The Chipko movement, which started in north India, was one of the key early environmental movements. Behind this movement is the notion of *shakti*, the sense of the active energy of the universe and of women that is so important in Hinduism. The participation of Indian women at the grass roots has been essential for this movement, which has engaged in protecting forests from lumber companies. One of the most eloquent environmental activists in India, Vandana Shiva, cites the Chipko movement as central to her early activism.

We can also celebrate the fact that Wangari Maathai won the Nobel Peace Prize in 2004 for her work as founder of the Green Belt Movement in Kenya. There she has empowered thousands of women to plant millions of trees over several decades now. This was the first time the Nobel Peace Prize was given to an environmentalist. Thus an important consequence of Wangari's Nobel award is that from here on peace and security are recognized as inextricably linked with ecological security and ecological integrity of ecosystems—without these conditions war and conflict are much more likely to break out. The United Nations Environment Programme and many of the United Nations' departments are acknowledging this reality in the conferences they are sponsoring.

Wangari, too, is making this connection that planetary peace depends on preserving the integrity of ecosystems.

We need even more women religious leaders, grassroots activists, and scholars of religion and theologians. We can identify and thank many of the ecofeminists, like Rosemary Ruether, Sallie McFague, Catherine Keller, Heather Eaton, and others. We should also note the work of ministers, such as Sally Bingham working at Grace Cathedral in San Francisco on the Regeneration Project for Episcopal Power and Light. Jewish leaders include Charlotte Fonrobert and Marcia Falk. Hava Tirosh-Samuelson has done remarkable scholarship in this area, including editing the volume *Judaism and Ecology: Created World and Revealed Word*.[3] In addition, Ellen Bernstein in her book *The Splendor of Creation* shows how Jewish ritual and spirituality connect with a sense of nature preservation and protection.[4]

I believe women clearly have something significant to contribute to this monumental global environmental and social crisis we are facing. Women's voices can be extremely helpful in reformulating human-Earth relations. I am not suggesting a simple essentialism of an identity between women and nature. Our voices range from tremendous ethical urgencies to broad aesthetic sensibilities that have not yet been expressed fully in a public context. These voices need to be heard for the benefit of future generations—for human children and the children of all species.

Women can continue to make contributions in at least three areas related to this crisis: reflecting on nature, articulating an ethic of relationality, and speaking out on environmental health issues. We need more artistic reflections on nature from women—on the impact of the seasons, of sunset, of dawn, of what it is that we feel in relationship to the vast transforming rhythms of the natural world. The profound feelings that we have with nature need to be lifted up, as they are often in poetry, in prose, in painting, and in nature writing. Nature writers, such as Terry Tempest Williams and Annie Dillard, and poets, such as Mary Oliver and Pattiann Rogers, have led the way in this regard.

We also need an ethic of relationality. Such an ethic is not just about the relations of humans to humans or humans to the divine, as important as those are. It is the relation of humans to the natural world that sustains us in numerous and mysterious ways. As Thomas Berry suggests, we humans have developed an ethic regarding homicide, suicide, and even genocide. These ethics are still, no doubt, inadequate and often not fully realized. But, Berry notes, we do not yet have an ethic that responds to biocide or ecocide. What does this say to those of us who bear and bring life to the world? Women carry an ethic of sustaining and giving *life*—biologically and physically in our bodies. What kind of ethics of relationality can we articulate in response to potential biocide or ecocide?

In this spirit, Caroline Merchant and Riane Eisler have called for a partnership ethic. There are many ways to describe such a partnership ethic, but they need to be lifted up into even greater visibility and practical application. Why is a partnership ethic of relationality so important? It is vital because stewardship ethics alone are not sufficient to respond to biocide or ecocide. Stewardship ethics still arise out of an anthropocentric rather than ecocentric or biocentric position.

Yet such an ethic beyond stewardship is emerging from unexpected sources. At the Baltic Sea Symposium, the leading Orthodox theologian, John of Pergamon, asked in his opening presentation, What does it mean for humans to live amid this environmental crisis? He pointed out that this is not just a question of the need for environmental stewardship. Rather, he said, the scale of the crisis calls for a change in the very ontology of the human. We need to ask, Who are we as humans? This comes from the leadership of the Greek Orthodox Church, which is conservative by some lights, but this is a radical and challenging notion for all of us. It is a powerful call for new human-Earth relations.

Women can also make contributions in terms of environmental health. What are we feeding our children? What can their bodies sustain? What is the relationship of the rise of various illnesses to environmental pollution? Women have important insights to contribute as they raise their children in an increasingly toxic and chemically saturated world.

Finally, I want to comment on the issue of women's roles in social and political movements, as we have seen throughout the twentieth century. What are we learning from the social and political changes that women have helped to create in dedicated ways yet with great opposition? Let us recall the difficulties of the women active in the suffrage movements of the early twentieth century. Now we are facing a similar task to protect the rights of the natural world and to establish a new basis for sustainable human-Earth relations. It is a significant challenge indeed.

Important openings are occurring right now in environmental discussions within the academy and beyond. The importance of ethics, values, and religion in creating lasting solutions to environmental problems is finally being recognized. Significantly, scientists and policy experts are inviting ethicists, theologians, and scholars of religion and religious leaders into these discussions. Over the last thirty years, not enough progress has been made in the environmental movement. Scientists say that we are at a turning point and that legislation and regulation are insufficient. Moreover, they observe that facts are not enough to change people's minds and to create new attitudes toward the environment. They note that climate change and environmental degradation are ethical issues. This new awareness can be seen in conferences in the United States such as the 2005 conference on global warming sponsored by the Yale Center for the Study of Globalization. Mikhail Gorbachev has chaired two major conferences in Europe in Lyon and Barcelona, called "Earth Dialogues: Is Ethics the Missing Link?" We know, from United Nations reports and others, that we have the facts, but we do not yet have the modes of spiritual and ethical transformation needed to take effective, long-term, sustained action.

An example of the changing attitude toward religion and the environment can be seen in the Worldwatch Institute's State of the World Report in 2003. The concluding chapter by Gary Gardner describes the growing efficacy of religion and ecology. This is a new departure for the environmental policy movement, which previously tended to see religion, ethics, and values as having no role in solving environmental problems. Another example is the work of the Stanford biologist and leading environmentalist Paul Ehrlich. In August 2004 he delivered a speech to the Ecological Society of America on the *Millennium Ecosystem Assessment*. Recognizing that science and policy still have not affected human behavior regarding the environment, he called for a "Millennium Assessment of Human Behavior." Ehrlich also cowrote an important article with the editor in chief of *Science* magazine, Donald Kennedy, making the case for such an assessment.[5] Ehrlich feels that this work needs the participation of those in the social sciences and humanities to reevaluate what is going to change and shift human behavior. What are the necessary ethical values to make this change to a sustainable future possible and practical?

What we need here is a broader sense of history. How do social and political movements effect change? For example, the abolitionist movement began in the nineteenth century, but it took a hundred years for the civil rights movement to emerge in the 1960s, and the struggle for civil rights is still ongoing. We can certainly say the same thing for feminism, which arose in the nineteenth century and moved slowly through the twentieth century. We still must analyze the modes of change and determine how women can participate more effectively in the process of change.

Science and policy are necessary but not sufficient for a robust environmental movement. A broader vision of human behavior and ethical values is developing. Social and political changes that women have been working on need to be brought into the environmental movement, and reflection on how those changes have taken place is absolutely critical. But above all—and I think this is the challenge we all face—it is absolutely essential that we learn to appreciate diversity in all areas—biological, cultural, and religious. And along with such appreciation we must create a sense of our common future, our dependence on the continuity of life on the planet.

Let me end with a challenging statement from Mihaly Csikszentmihalyi in his book *The Evolving Self*. He writes, "The only value that all humans can readily share is the continuation of life on Earth. In this one goal, all individual self interests are united. Unless such a species identity takes precedence over the more particular identities of faith, nation, family, or person, it will be difficult to agree on a course that must be taken to guarantee our future." My question is, How can we contribute to a species identification? He continues, "It is for this reason that the fate of humanity in the next millennium depends so closely on what kind of selves we will succeed in creating." And what kind of selves will we succeed in creating? "Evolution is by no means guaranteed," he observes.

"We have a chance of being part of it, only as long as we understand our place in that gigantic field of force called nature."[6]

That is our challenge: to find our place in the field of force we call nature. Let our multiple voices come into this conversation in powerful and transforming ways.

CHAPTER NINE

Prayer as Poetry, Poetry as Prayer: A Liturgist's Exploration

Marcia Falk

PREFATORY REMARKS

Some cultures pray with silence and some with song, some with meditative stillness and some with ecstatic movement. In considering the relationship between poetry and prayer, I am speaking about only one of many modes: praying with words, with human speech.

What does poetry have to do with prayer? The very question reveals something about Western culture in our time, something that sets us off from earlier civilizations. In the ancient world, the arts expressed sacrality; today we tend to think of religion and art as existing in separate—if not competing—realms. Poets are not expected to create sacred texts; liturgists are not assumed to be poets. But does this separation hold up when thinking about the creative process, the creative life? I'm not convinced it does.

The question, "What does poetry have to do with prayer?" is one that comes up when I speak about my liturgical work, *The Book of Blessings*, which re-creates Jewish prayer in poetic forms. I have been asked more than once to explain why and how this prayer book emerged as a compilation of poems (or how a compilation of poems came to be a prayer book). To my astonishment, I have even been asked why each blessing is given its own page, as is customary with books of poetry (rather than each page being crammed with as many words as possible, as in a tractate of Talmud). Yet despite the frequency with which it arises, the question, "What does poetry have to do with prayer?" always strikes me as somewhat redundant. Prayer as poetry, poetry as prayer—the connection seems self-evident. Even in today's postmodern world, when the meaning of "meaning" is up for grabs, surely many poets strive for a kind of transcendence, a wholeness that is larger than the self, a truth that can be expressed only in intensified language—in other words, something sacred. The word *sacred*, of course, is highly charged, and many artists would not choose it to describe what they are after in their work. Other words—such as *truth*, *meaning*, *beauty*—are more likely to arise in discussions of the artistic process. But though the terms may not be the same as in previous eras, the model of the poet as prophet, and of poetry as sacred text, is not completely outdated.

Some might argue that prayer has specific functions that do not necessarily apply to poetry. For example, in Judaism (the tradition I know best) the recitation of a blessing brings attention to a moment in time, setting it off, "consecrating" it. Some blessings convey hopes and petitions; some express gratitude and appreciation; still others are a form of exultation. Some prayers induce reflectiveness; some evoke a state of wonder. And though we may not automatically associate it with the political realm, prayer can at times articulate ethical, social, and political values and commitments.

But poems, too, can play all of these roles, depending on the context in which they are recited, performed, or read. For some readers the main difference between poetry and prayer comes down to use: poetry may become prayer when it is spoken or read in particular places at particular times. Intentionality, too, plays a part; how the speaker or reader (not necessarily the poet) intends the words to be received can also turn a poem into a prayer.

Embedded in this discussion is a critical question I have not yet addressed: Can poems be considered prayers if they do not speak directly to God as "Other"? The answer, of course, depends on how one defines both prayer and God. For those of us who sense the divine as *inherent* in the world—that is, as something inseparable from us, which cannot be addressed as an Other—it may be impossible to pray by speaking *to* God. And yet many of us would say we have experiences of prayer. I have prayerful moments when I am alone in nature or when I am in the presence of great art—painting, sculpture, music, dance, poetry. Sometimes, when reading a poem, I find myself entering it deeply, becoming wholly absorbed in its world. This union, which I do not so much *make* happen as *allow* to happen, is, for me, a kind of prayer. Another way I might say this is that a poem becomes a prayer when I let it speak both to me and for me.

But why poetry, rather than other verbal modes? Poetry has been described as an intensified form of language, and this intensification is in large measure the result of words being laid out *in lines.* The visual image a poem makes on the page is not only, not even primarily, a mere pictorial representation; it is, foremost, a guide to the poem's oral expression. The words that make up the line—the black ink on the page—indicate sound; the white space at the end of each line denotes a pause, which is to say, silence. Together, the sound and the silence create music and sense; when handled well, the melding of content and form yields elegant expression.

Does all prayer have, or need, this kind of elegance? The truth is that traditional prayer varies a great deal in this regard: in Jewish liturgy, for example, one finds gemlike blessings sprinkled among rambling and repetitious passages; formal, finely crafted *piyyutim* (liturgical poems by a single author) are set alongside blocks of tedious prose. Yet this mixture says more about what gets canonized than about what truly engages the mind and the heart. I believe that what applies to poetry also applies to prayer: if its language is not eloquent, if its form does not echo its meaning, it is less likely to realize its potential to deepen the human experience.

MY STORY, PART ONE

Virtually all my experiences with prayer have been as a Jew; I have been *davvening* (Yiddish for "praying") with the traditional Jewish prayer book since I was a young child. At one point in my thirties, however, I found myself no longer able to pray using that book. Not only did the words not meet my spiritual needs, but the patriarchal language, imagery, and themes—in particular, the repeated exaltations and adorations of the "Lord-God-King-of-the-world"—were disturbing, even enraging.

I was not alone in my discomfort. I eventually discovered other Jews, especially Jewish feminists, who were as troubled as I was by the exclusive representation of divinity as Lord-God-King. Over the course of the past three decades, Jewish feminists have taken the lead in addressing this issue, bringing a wholly fresh perspective into Jewish liturgical life. Unwilling to choose between our feminism and our Judaism, refusing to give up either the integrity of our speech or our attachment to our people's history, we have called for new prayers that express our convictions in a Jewish idiom. And indeed, liturgical revisions and innovations have been appearing with greater and greater frequency in English (and, to some extent, in other diaspora languages), so that today it is common to see individual synagogues producing their own prayer books or supplements to the standard prayer books. But outside of Israel—and there, only sporadically—few attempts are being made to compose new liturgy in Hebrew, the ancient and universal language of Judaism, the language Jews call the "holy tongue." The reason is obvious: few diaspora Jews have intimate knowledge of the Hebrew language and sufficient acquaintance with Hebrew literature to write in it authentically and richly. The majority of diaspora Jews, in fact, do not know Hebrew at all, and those who do—those who know modern Hebrew well enough to write in it and who are also well-versed in the long history of Hebrew liturgical tradition—tend to come from strict religious backgrounds, making them less likely to be interested in changing or updating prayer.

MY STORY, PART TWO

For reasons I am at a loss to fully explain, I fell in love with the Hebrew language when I was a child, and the love affair has continued ever since. Despite the fact that it was not my first language, I have always considered Hebrew to be my rightful inheritance—the language of my origins, if not my mother tongue. This attachment led me to study Hebrew literature throughout my life. At the same time, I have loved English poetry for as long as I have been a reader, and I have been practicing its craft for much of my life as well. In the 1970s I set out to unite these twin passions by interpreting and translating the love poetry of the Bible, the Song of Songs. I sought to create an English rendition that would open up the metaphors and suggest the musicality of the ancient text, allowing it to come alive to English-speaking audiences in our time. I was drawn to the Song for many reasons, in particular, its exquisite lyricism and sensuality, its preponderance of female speakers, and the mutuality it expressed between female and male voices and between the human domain and the rest of the natural world. As a collection of folk poetry, orally composed, the Song is the only biblical book to which women surely contributed authorship. In all these ways, it is not only unique in the Hebrew Bible but an invaluable resource for Jewish women seeking connections to our earliest sources and traditions.

When I completed my translation of the Song (it was first published in 1977 and remains in print today), I was determined to continue translating Hebrew poetry. I sought other biblical texts that, like the Song, presented women's speech unmediated by a male narrator, speech that may actually have been composed by women. Sadly, I was soon to discover that none exist. I turned to the postbiblical era, but even there, until the nineteenth century, few texts by Jewish women are to be found, and the few that are extant are not literary in nature. The late-nineteenth and twentieth centuries, however, contain a treasure trove of Hebrew and Yiddish poetry by women, most of it unknown to English readers. I determined to carry some of those voices over into an English idiom, to give them exposure to a broader audience.

For several years, that was where my feminist grappling with Judaism remained. I did not enter into Talmudic debates about theology; I was uninterested in changing *halakhah* (Jewish law). And I certainly did not plan to compose liturgy of any kind. For one thing, I did not (do not) embrace a personal God, and the image of the deity in Jewish prayer is consistently anthropomorphic—this despite the fact that Jewish philosophers emphasize that all anthropomorphizing is a fiction, the compromise we must make to speak about divinity in human language. For me, talking to God as though God were a person is only perpetuating a lie. Indeed, talking to God at all—which is what I once believed to be the definition of prayer—feels unnatural to me.

Still, my experience of belonging to a greater whole—a whole to which we all belong and for which we all share responsibility—called out to me increasingly over the years, and I wanted to give it expression through poetry, as a *Jewish* poet. The thirteen-year project that culminated in 1996 in the publication of *The Book of Blessings* began as a relatively small step toward correcting what I saw as the imbalances and distortions of Judaism's patriarchal imagery. At the outset, I only intended to create several new Hebrew blessings to be used in place of the old ones. I started by rewriting the traditional blessing form, replacing the rabbinic image of *adonay eloheynu melekh ha'olam*, "Lord our God, King of the world," with new images for the divine, such as *eyn haḥayim*, "the wellspring of life." I also changed the voice of the traditional blessing from the passive phrasing of *barukh atah*, "Thou [masculine] art blessed," to the active, gender-inclusive exhortation *n'varekh*, "Let us bless." Thus, instead of *barukh atah adonay eloheynu melekh ha'olam*, "Blessed are you, Lord our God, King of the world," my new blessings opened with the phrase *n'varekh et eyn haḥayim*, "Let us bless the source of life." This phrasing was intended to shift the focus away from God's otherness and toward the community of speakers, in an acknowledgment that it is we who are responsible for sacralizing the moments of our lives.

It was never my aim to create new formulas to substitute for the old. ("No surprise for the writer," wrote Robert Frost, "no surprise for the reader"—and who wants a book without surprise?) So after a while I began to experiment with a variety of poetic genres to express different liturgical themes. And I began to think about including voices besides my own in my liturgy, because I felt that no single voice could reflect the full diversity of the community for which I was writing. Thus the poems by Jewish women that I had been reading and translating for years entered the body of liturgical work I found myself creating.

Over the course of more than a decade, *The Book of Blessings* changed shape many times, even as my theology sharpened its focus and evolved. (The creative process influenced the spiritual journey as much as the other way around.) All the while, the slender volume I had set out to produce kept expanding. Eventually I saw that I was writing a *siddur*—a Jewish prayer book—something I never set out to do.

I didn't intend it; it just seemed to happen. My love of Hebrew, my commitment to Jewish feminism, and, perhaps more than anything else, my need to write poems—all these joined together and led me to become a liturgist. Writing prayer as poetry, poetry as prayer, I no longer saw a clear difference between the two modes.

Here is a look at some of the poetry that became—to no one's surprise more than my own—a book of prayer.[1]

WOMEN'S LYRICS AS PSALMS

Kabbalat Shabbat, the service that welcomes the Sabbath on Friday evenings, is a relatively recent addition to rabbinic prayer, having been composed by Kabbalists in Safed, Israel, at the end of the sixteenth century. The liturgy for Sabbath eve focuses thematically on the creation of the universe, and at the center of the kabbalistic service is a sequence of biblical psalms celebrating the creator and the creation. In the re-creation of the *Kabbalat Shabbat* that appears in *The Book of Blessings*, the biblical psalms are replaced with poems of the natural world written by Jewish women of the last two centuries. Instead of praising the creator of the world, these latter-day psalms explore our relationship as human beings to the greater whole of creation. "Psalms of Creation," as I entitle this selection, is divided into four parts: "Alone, and at One"; "The Healing of the Wind"; "The River and the Sea"; "The Earth and Its Fullness." Below are excerpts from each part.

From "Alone, and at One," here is a poem of solitude and union by the twentieth-century Hebrew mystic Zelda:

The Golden Butterfly
When the golden butterfly wends its way
through a river of colors and scents
toward its flower-mate, and clings
as though this flower were the star
of its secret self—
an inexplicable clamor of hope
rises in every heart.

And when that beautiful flutterer
abandons the weary petals
and vanishes in space,
the lonely moment wakens in the world,
a soul vanishes in infinity.

From "The Healing of the Wind," here is a meditative poem by the Yiddish poet Anna Margolin:

Slender Ships

Slender ships drowse on swollen green water,
black shadows sleep on the cold heart of water.
All the winds are still.
Clouds shift like ghosts in the speechless night.
The earth, pale and calm, awaits lightning and thunder.
I will be still.

Here is one of my own poems, included in "The Healing of the Wind":

We Know Her

We see her in the shimmering blades,
their bright green waving on the hill,

and hear her through the cottonwoods, the birches,
flying free through their leafy crowns.

We breathe her as she lifts to the sky
the scents of the newly-furrowed field,

and feel her touching our forehead
in our fevered dreams.

Only her taste is saved
for tomorrow—

the dark taste of her emptiness,
remembered honey of mother's milk—

manna of our longing,
wind.

"The River and the Sea" contains two poems from the sequence "Songs of the River" by the great modern Hebrew poet Leah Goldberg:

The Blade of Grass
Sings to the River

Even for the little ones like me,
one among the throng,
for the children of poverty
on disappointment's shores,
the river hums its song,
lovingly hums its song.

The sun's gentle caress
touches it now and then,
and I, too, am reflected
in waters that flow green,
and in the river's depths
each one of us is deep.

My ever-deepening image
streaming away to the sea
is swallowed up, erased
on the edge of vanishing.
And with the river's voice,
the ever-silent soul,
with the river's psalm,
sings praises of the world.

The River Sings to the Stone

I kissed the stone in the cold of her dream,
for she is the silence and I am the psalm;
she is the riddle and I the riddler,
the two of us cut from one eternity.

I kissed the solitary flesh of the stone.
She, the sworn faithful, and I who betray,
she, the enduring, and I who pass on,
she, the earth's secrets, and I who tell all.

And I knew, when I touched a speechless heart:
I am the poet and she is the world.

"The Earth and Its Fullness"—the last section of the "Psalms of Creation"—includes a poem by the innovative American Yiddish modernist Malka Heifetz Tussman, in which an empathetic moment yields an epiphany:

Last Apple

"I am the last apple
that falls from the tree
and no one picks up."

I kneel to the fragrance
of the last apple
and I pick it up.

In my hands—the tree,
in my hands—the leaf,
in my hands—the blossom,
and in my hands—the earth
that kisses the apple
that no one picks up.

Should the various poems cited above be considered prayer? None was written specifically for that purpose. And yet, read silently or spoken aloud as part of the Sabbath eve service, they can awaken wonder and imbue serenity—qualities that are at the heart of a prayerful Sabbath experience. I have seen it happen, many times.

PRAYER AS POETIC COLLAGE

In another section of *The Book of Blessings*, I was challenged to find a way to re-create a lengthy, multipart rabbinic prayer, the *Amidah*. Referred to in the Talmud as the "prayer of the heart," the *Amidah* is the mainstay of most synagogue services. To re-create it, I had to find a structure that could sustain length and contain recurrent motifs without becoming tediously repetitive. I settled on a kind of poetic collage, in which the various elements of the prayer would be represented with different poetic forms.

Based on the traditional Sabbath *Amidah*, which has seven sections, the *Amidah* in *The Book of Blessings* also has seven sections, each of which re-speaks the theme of its traditional counterpart. The structure is the same for all sections. Each opens with a prose poem, which is followed by a blessing in Hebrew and a parallel blessing in English, then a series of lyric poems (once again, by a variety of Jewish women). After the last poem in the section, the blessing is reprised and capped by a two-line refrain—the same refrain for all seven sections. Each of the genres serves a different function: the prose poem acts as a meditation to focus awareness, the blessings encapsulate the theme, the lyric poems elaborate on the theme, and the refrain ties the section to the rest of the *Amidah*. As with the "Psalms of Creation," none of the lyric poems in this new *Amidah* was originally written to be used as prayer. And yet, set in this context, each plays a role in the prayer experience that is no less central than that of the blessings and meditations. The ways in the different poetic genres are used to explore theological themes is perhaps best demonstrated with a part-by-part presentation of one section of the prayer.

The second section of my *Amidah* grapples with a particularly challenging passage in the liturgy, the blessing of God as "reviver of the dead." This attribute of the divine is viewed as problematic among many liberal Jews today; both the Reform and Reconstructionist movements of Judaism have eliminated references to God as "reviver of the dead" in recent versions of their prayer books (substituting euphemisms such as "reviver of all" and "reviver of all that lives"). Although one can understand the difficulty a modern worshiper might have with Ezekiel's vision of God inspiriting the dry bones and resurrecting the dead from their graves, it nevertheless seems an error to entirely expunge reference to the dead from this section of the liturgy. For one thing, this is the primary moment in the synagogue service that deals with death, and for another, the theme of revival of the dead is not, I would argue, any more problematic or less open to metaphorical interpretation than many other traditional themes (most of which are left intact in the non-Orthodox movements' prayer books). Rather, I believe it is part of the Jewish feminist enterprise to reconceptualize rabbinic theology, including the concept of revival, in ways that speak to us honestly and meaningfully. This is what I attempted to do in the section of my *Amidah* titled "Sustaining Life, Embracing Death."

It opens with this meditation:

To celebrate life is to acknowledge the ongoing dying, and ultimately to embrace death. For although all life travels toward its death, death is not a destination: it too is a journey to beginnings: all death leads to life again. From peelings to mulch to new potatoes, the world is ever-renewing, ever-renewed.

Next comes the blessing, which, in both the Hebrew and the English versions, takes the form of a rhymed quatrain, mirroring life folding back on itself, endings connecting with beginnings:

N'varekh et hama'yan
adey-ad m'fakeh—
ma'gal hahayim
hamemit um'hayeh.

Let us bless the well
eternally giving—
the circle of life
ever-dying, ever-living.

The blessing is followed by poems in three languages—Yiddish, Hebrew, and English. This poem by Leah Goldberg depicts death, with a light touch, as an inseparable part of everyday living:

In Everything
In everything, there is at least an eighth
of death.
It doesn't weigh much.
With what hidden, peaceful charm
we carry it everywhere we go.
In sweet awakenings,
in our travels,
in our love talk,
when we are unaware,
forgotten in all the corners of our being—
always with us.
And never heavy.

Another poem, by Malka Heifetz Tussman, emphasizes the theme of never-ending cycles through its use of the triolet form, in which the opening two lines are repeated at the end:

Leaves

Leaves don't fall. They descend.
Longing for earth, they come winging.
In their time, they'll come again,
For leaves don't fall. They descend.
On the branches, they will be again
Green and fragrant, cradle-swinging,
For leaves don't fall. They descend.
Longing for earth, they come winging.

The last poems in this section are my own:

Winter Solstice 1

Here you are, back
in the blue-white woods—

how tall the birches,
how delicate the pines!

Standing on the frozen plot of snow,
you suddenly know these trees

will be your gravestone.
Nothing stirs—but what

are those sounds?
You balance on the crusty edge

while all around you ice
invisibly thaws,

beneath the snow
the mushrooms smolder,

and under your feet the unborn grass
hums in its bed.

Winter Solstice 2

Warm breeze across the winter sky,
the birch trunk shedding its skin,
ice beginning to give beneath your feet—

It's alive, alive beneath the stillness,
under the frozen surface of the pond,
in the moss-webbed rock, alive!

In the unseen hoof of the deer
whose quick track lightly pierced the snow,
and in all the unnamed footprints,

and in all the longed-for music
of the last dead leaves
and the still-twittering birds, alive!

And in the bronze of the inert star
that melts the snow
and erases the deer tracks,

and turns wet skin to parchment,
flesh to fossil, water to stone
again—

After the selection of lyrics, the blessing is reprised, and the section closes with the refrain that unites all seven sections of the *Amidah*:

N'varekh et eyn hahayim
v'khoh nitbarekh.

As we bless the source of life,
so we are blessed.

Although I refer to my re-creation of the *Amidah* as a collage of poetic forms, I do not think of it as a finished collage. The variety of genres and styles implies, I hope, that there is room for other forms and other voices—room for the pray-er to add the prayer of her or his own heart.

IN CLOSING, I LET
THE BIBLICAL PSALMIST MAKE MY CASE

I conclude with what is perhaps the most controversial passage in *The Book of Blessings*—a re-creation of the traditional *Sh'ma, Yisra'el* ("Hear, O Israel"). The *Sh'ma* is without doubt the most well-known prayer in Judaism; sometimes referred to as Judaism's "keynote," it articulates the sine qua non of Jewish faith: belief in a monotheistic God. Many of my readers were shocked that I had dared to rewrite this most sacred of all sacred texts. Yet, given its importance, how could I have omitted it?

What is fascinating to me about the traditional *Sh'ma* is that it is not, in fact, an I-Thou dialogue. That is, it is not spoken *to* God; rather, it is a compilation of passages, from Deuteronomy and Numbers, addressed to an individual human (male) hearer. It commands loyalty to, and love for, a single deity, and it enumerates specific commandments that follow from this love. That it is considered a prayer at all establishes, I believe, a basis for expanding the definition of prayer to include other modes besides the direct address of God.

In my version of the *Sh'ma*, I reenvision monotheism as an inclusive embracing of multiplicity and diversity within the oneness of all creation. The affirmation of this oneness is followed by a reconception of the idea of commandment. Instead of positing an external commander who demands love and obedience, to be expressed through the performance of specific ritual acts, this new *Sh'ma* sets forth moral commitments that derive from core Jewish values—values that are also harmonious with a feminist ethic. Not just the themes but much of the language in this re-creation are adapted from classical (primarily biblical) Jewish sources.

The prayer ends with a quotation taken not from the original *Sh'ma* but from Psalms. To my mind, Ps. 85:11 not only is one of the most exquisite verses in all poetry but aptly demonstrates the power of poetry to become quintessential prayer. In re-creating the *Sh'ma*, I aspired to compose a poem—a prayer—worthy of concluding with the psalmist's words.

Sh'ma:
Communal Declaration
of Faith

Hear, O Israel—
The divine abounds everywhere
and dwells in everything;
the many are One.

_____

Loving life
and its mysterious source
with all our heart
and all our spirit,
all our senses and strength,
we take upon ourselves
and into ourselves
these promises:
to care for the earth
and those who live upon it,
to pursue justice and peace,
to love kindness and compassion.
We will teach this to our children
throughout the passage of the day—
as we dwell in our homes
and we go on our journeys,
from the time we rise
until we fall asleep.
And may our actions
be faithful to our words
that our children's children
may live to know:
Truth and kindness
have embraced,
peace and justice have kissed
and are one.

Notes

Introduction

1. The GTU is a consortium of nine theological seminaries, Catholic and Protestant: the American Baptist Seminary of the West, the Church Divinity School of the Pacific (Episcopalian), the Dominican School of Philosophy and Theology, the Franciscan School of Theology, the Jesuit School of Theology at Berkeley, the Pacific Lutheran Theological Seminary, the Pacific School of Religion (United Church of Christ), the San Francisco Theological Seminary (Presbyterian), and the Starr King School for the Ministry (Unitarian-Universalist). The GTU also includes several affiliated centers: the Richard S. Dinner Center for Jewish Studies, the Institute of Buddhist Studies, the Patriarch Athenagoras Orthodox Institute, and the Center for Theology and the Natural Sciences.

Chapter 1: The History of the Center

1. The author would like to thank Pamela Cooper-White, Clare Fischer, China Galland, Lucinda Glenn, Mary E. Hunt, Maureen Maloney, and Barbara Waugh for their contributions.

2. Inna Jane Ray and Cheryl A. Kirk-Duggan, eds., "The Atonement Muddle: An Historical Analysis and Clarification of a Salvation Theory," *Journal of Women and Religion* 15 (1997): 1–36.

3. Mary E. Hunt, *Fierce Tenderness: A Feminist Theology of Friendship* (New York: Crossroad, 1991); Patricia Beattie Jung, Mary E. Hunt, and Radhika Balakrishnan, eds., *Good Sex: Feminist Perspectives from the World's Religions* (New Brunswick, NJ: Rutgers Univ. Press, 2001); Mary E. Hunt, ed., *A Guide for Women and Religion: Making Your Way from A to Z* (New York: Palgrave Macmillan, 2004).

4. Barbara Waugh with Margot Silk Forrest, *The Soul in the Computer: The Story of a Corporate Revolutionary* (Maui, HI: Inner Ocean, 2001).

5. Nelle Morton, *The Journey Is Home* (Boston: Beacon, 1985).

6. China Galland, *Longing for Darkness: Tara and the Black Madonna: A Ten-Year Journey* (New York: Viking, 1990).

7. "Lifting others as we climb" is a phrase often used in the African American community; for example, when it was founded in 1896, the National Association of Colored Women's Clubs used it as its motto.

8. Lynn Rhodes, *Co-Creating: A Feminist Vision of Ministry* (Louisville: Westminster John Knox, 1987).

9. Mary E. Hunt, ed., *From Woman Pain to Woman Vision: Writings in Feminist Theology* (Minneapolis: Fortress Press, 1989).

10. Antoinette Clark Wire, *The Corinthian Women Prophets: A Reconstruction through Paul's Rhetoric* (Minneapolis: Fortress Press, 1990).

11. Rosemary Chinnici, *Can Women Re-Image the Church?* (New York: Paulist, 1992).

12. Martha Ellen Stortz, *PastorPower* (Nashville: Abingdon, 1993).

13. Valerie DeMarinis, *Critical Caring: A Feminist Model for Pastoral Psychotherapy* (Louisville: Westminster John Knox, 1994).

14. Pamela Cooper-White, *The Cry of Tamar: Violence Against Women and the Church's Response* (Minneapolis: Fortress Press, 1995).

15. Jane Spahr, Kathryn Poethig, and Melinda McLain, eds., *Called Out: The Voices and Gifts of Lesbian, Gay, Bisexual and Transgendered Presbyterians* (Gaithersburg, MD: Chi Rho, 1995).

16. Til Evans and Pamela Cooper-White, "Ambiguity, Diversity and Risk: CWR's Position in the GTU," *CWR Membership Newsletter*, September 1993, 1.

17. Ibid., 3.

18. Ibid., 4.

19. Citing bell hooks's *Feminist Theory: From Margin to Center* (Boston: South End, 1984).

20. James Marcia, et al., *Ego Identity: A Handbook for Psychosocial Research* (New York: Springer, 1993).

21. Jean Baker Miller, *Toward a New Psychology of Women*, 2nd ed. (Boston: Beacon, 1987).

22. See, for example, Judith Jordan et al., *Women's Growth in Connection: Writings from the Stone Center* (New York: Guilford, 1991).

23. Evans and Cooper-White, "Ambiguity, Diversity and Risk," 3–4.

24. Leroy Wells Jr., "The Group-as-a-Whole Perspective and Its Theoretical Roots," *Group Relations Reader 2*, ed. Arthur Coleman and Marvin Geller (Sausalito, CA: A. K. Rice Institute, 1985), 114–17, cited in Wally Fletcher, "The Bishop and the Hack: Dealing with Countertransference Hate in a Case of Modern Psychoanalytic Consultancy," presented at the International Society for the Psychoanalytic Study of Organizations 2005 Symposium, Baltimore, MD. See also Wilfred Bion, *Experience in Groups* (New York: Ballantine; London: Tavistock, 1961), 147.

25. Melanie Klein, *The Writings of Melanie Klein*, vol. 3 *Envy and Gratitude and Other Works 1946–1963*, (New York: Free Press, 1984).

26. Bion, *Experiences in Groups*.

27. These thoughts were first presented in a conference at the Graduate Theological Union on critical world views in 2000.

28. Harold S. Kushner, *When Bad Things Happen to Good People* (New York: Random House, 1981, 1990).

29. Here we must also recognize other immigrants from South America who may appear Hispanic or part of the African diaspora but who speak Portuguese and indigenous languages.

30. Quoted in "Daily Almanac, 7/10/02," *Naomi's New Morning*, http://www.newmorningtv.tv/dailyalmanac_071002.jsp.

Chapter 2: Pacific and Asian Women's Theologies

1. Pronounced pan-autumn. For a history of the organization, see www.panaawtm.org.

2. The excerpt is from "The Future of PANAAWTM Theology," written by Kwok Pui Lan, Seung Ai Yang, and myself in early July 2004, using an innovative Internet technology called "Synanim" (*syn* = together, synchronous, and *anima*, *animus* = spirit or mind). We were the first people to test Synanim, and we posted the paper on our Web site. In March 2005, thousands of people nationwide used Synanim to write a declaration to end the Iraq War. PANAAWTM thus contributed in a small way to what became a sixty-five-member coalition of groups representing millions of people supporting work for peace and justice. The complete PANAAWTM document is available at www.panaawtm.org under "Resources."

Information about Synanim and documents written with it are available at http://www.synanim.org under "Programs."

3. Material for this section is taken from research Rebecca Parker and I have done for a book, *Saving Paradise*, forthcoming in 2007 from Beacon Press.

4. Georges Florovsky, *The Eastern Fathers of the Fourth Century*, vol. 7, trans. Catherine Edmunds (Vaduz, Europa: Büchervertriebsanstalt, 1987), provides an extensive discussion of *theosis*. Quote from Gregory of Nyssa is found in Kilian McDonnell, *The Baptism of Jesus in the Jordan: The Trinitarian and Cosmic Order of Salvation* (Collegeville, MN: Liturgical Press, 1996), 129. While many early church fathers turned directly to Greek philosophical ideas to describe *theosis*, Ephrem of Syria used scriptures such as 2 Peter 1:1-4; Eph. 4:22-24; John 1:42; 15:4; 17:22-23; and Rom. 6:5; 8:14-17 (128–44). Ephrem's use of images such as glory, fire, water, and a robe of light shares much with Samaritan religious ideas, which relied on the Moses tradition and paralleled the Moses-Logos traditions of the Gospel of John (*pace* Rita Nakashima Brock and Rebecca Parker).

5. McDonnell, *The Baptism of Jesus*, 129.

6. Virginia Burrus, *Begotten, Not Made: Conceiving Manhood in Late Antiquity* (Stanford: Stanford Univ. Press, 2000), 3.

7. St. Ephrem the Syrian, *Hymns on Paradise*, ed. and trans. Sebastian Brock (Crestwood, NY: St. Vladimir's Seminary Press, 1990), 73–74.

8. Hymn 22:2-21 in *Ephrem the Syrian: Hymns*, trans. Kathleen E. McVey, Classics of Western Spirituality (New York: Paulist, 1989), 355–57.

9. Ibid., 431, 455.

10. Robert Louis Wilken, *The Spirit of Early Christian Thought: Seeking the Face of God* (New Haven, CT: Yale Univ. Press, 2003), 21.

Chapter 3: Latinas Writing Theology

1. Ada María Isasi-Díaz, "Toward an Understanding of Feminismo Hispano in the U.S.A.," in *Women's Consciousness, Women's Conscience: A Reader in Feminist Ethics*, ed. Barbara Hilkert Andolsen, Christine E. Gudorf, and Mary D. Pellauer (Minneapolis: Winston, 1985), 51.

2. Juana Inés de la Cruz, *A Woman of Genius: The Intellectual Autobiography of Sor Juana Inés de la Cruz*, ed. and trans. Margaret Sayers Peden (Salisbury, CT: Lime Rock, 1982), 26.

3. Michelle A. Gonzalez, *Sor Juana: Beauty and Justice in the Americas* (Maryknoll, NY: Orbis Books, 2003); Pamela Kirk, *Sor Juana Inés de la Cruz: Religion, Art, and Feminism* (New York: Continuum, 1998); Stephanie Merrim, ed., *Feminist Perspectives on Sor Juana Inés de la Cruz* (Detroit: Wayne State Univ. Press, 1991).

4. Charlotte Whaley, *Nina Otero-Warren of Santa Fe* (Albuquerque: Univ. of New Mexico Press, 1994); Cleofas M. Jaramillo, *Sombras del Pasado: Shadows of the Past* (Santa Fe: Ancient City, 1941); Fabiola Cabeza de Baca, *We Fed Them Cactus* (Albuquerque: Univ. of New Mexico Press, 1954).

5. Vicki L. Ruiz, *From Out of the Shadows: Mexican Women in Twentieth-Century America* (New York: Oxford Univ. Press, 1998), 91; Elizabeth Salas, "Adelina Otero Warren: Rural Aristocrat and Modern Feminist," in *Latina Legacies: Identity, Biography, and Community*, ed. Vicki L. Ruiz and Virginia Sánchez Korrol (New York: Oxford Univ. Press, 2005), 135–47; Whaley, *Nina Otero-Warren of Santa Fe*.

6. Norma Alarcón, "Tradutora, Traditora: A Paradigmatic Figure of Chicana Feminism," in *Scattered Hegemonies: Postmodernity and Transnational Feminist Practices*, ed. Inderpal Grewal and Caren Kaplan (Minneapolis: Univ. of Minnesota Press, 1994), 129–30.

7. Gloria Anzaldúa, *Borderlands/La Frontera: The New Mestiza* (San Francisco: Spinsters/Aunt Lute, 1987), 84, 78.

8. Gloria Anzaldúa, *Interviews = Entrevistas/Gloria Anzaldúa*, ed. AnaLouise Keating (New York: Routledge, 2000), 220–21.

9. Ibid., 9–11, 180, 282.

10. Anzaldúa, *Borderlands/La Frontera*, 79.

11. Chéla Sandoval, "Mestizaje as Method: Feminists-of-Color Challenge the Canon," in *Living Chicana Theory*, ed. Carla Trujillo (Berkeley, CA: Third Woman, 1998), 356.

12. Ibid., 356.

13. Laura Elisa Pérez, "El Desorden, Nationalism and Chicana/o Aesthetics," in *BetweenWoman and Nation: Nationalism, Transnational Feminisms, and the State*, ed. Caren Kaplan, et al. (Durham, NC: Duke Univ. Press, 1999), 19–46.

14. Sandoval, "Mestizaje as Method," 360; Pérez, "El Desorden."

15. Sandoval, "Mestizaje as Method," 362; Chéla Sandoval, *Methodology of the Oppressed* (Minneapolis: Univ. of Minnesota Press, 2000).

16. Cherríe Moraga, *The Last Generation: Prose and Poetry* (Boston: South End, 1993), 158.

17. Norma Alarcón, "Chicana's Feminist Literature: A Re-vision through Malintzin, or Malintzin: Putting Flesh Back on the Object," in *This Bridge Called My Back: Writings by Radical Women of Color*, ed. Cherríe Moraga and Gloria Anzaldúa, 2nd ed. (New York: Kitchen Table: Women of Color Press, 1983), 189.

18. Alarcón, "Tradutora, Traditora," 113 (emphasis added).

Chapter 4: Womanist Theology and Ethics

1. Alice Walker, *In Search of Our Mothers' Gardens* (San Diego: Harcourt Brace Jovanovich, 1983), xi–xii.

2. Linda J. M. La Rue, "Black Liberation and Women's Lib," *Trans-Action* (November–December, 1970): 61, cited in Paula Giddings, *When and Where I Enter: The Impact of Black Women on Race and Sex in America* (New York: Bantam, 1984), 308.

3. Toni Morrison, "What the Black Woman Thinks about Women's Lib," *New York Times Magazine*, August 22, 1971, 15, cited in Giddings, *When and Where I Enter*, 308.

4. Katie Geneva Cannon, *Katie's Canon: Womanism and the Soul of the Black Community* (New York: Continuum, 1995), 23–24.

5. Joan M. Martin, *More Than Chains and Toil: A Christian Work Ethic of Enslaved Black Women* (Louisville: Westminster John Knox, 2000).

6. Marcia Y. Riggs, *Plenty Good Room: Women Versus Male Power in the Black Church* (Cleveland: Pilgrim, 2003).

7. Cannon, *Katie's Canon*, 23.

8. Gloria T. Hull, Patricia Bell-Scott, and Barbara Smith, *All the Women Were White, All the Blacks Were Men, But Some of Us Were Brave* (Old Westbury, NY: Feminist Press, 1982).

9. Toni Morrison, "Home," in *The House That Race Built: Black Americans, U.S. Terrain*, ed. Wahneema Lubiano (New York: Pantheon Books, 1997), 3.

10. Marcia Y. Riggs, *Awake, Arise, and Act: A Womanist Call for Black Liberation* (Cleveland: Pilgrim, 1994).

11. James Cone, *Risks of Faith: The Emergence of a Black Theology of Liberation, 1968–1998* (Boston: Beacon, 1999), 135.

12. Kelly Brown Douglas, *Sexuality and the Black Church: A Womanist Perspective* (Maryknoll, NY: Orbis Books, 1999).

Chapter 5: Unfinished Business

1. Among Rosemary Radford Ruether's dozens of books are *Women and Redemption: A Theological History* (Minneapolis: Fortress Press, 1998), and *Christianity and the Making of the Modern Family* (Boston: Beacon, 2000).

2. Elisabeth Schüssler Fiorenza, *But She Said: Feminist Practices of Biblical Interpretation* (Boston: Beacon, 1992), 8.

3. First Interamerican Symposium on Feminist Intercultural Theology, http://www.sandiego.edu/theo/Latino-Cath/feminttheo.php.

4. Diana L. Eck, "Neighboring Faiths," *Harvard Magazine*, September–October 1996, 44.

5. Mary E. Hunt, "Sexual Integrity," *WATERwheel* 7, no. 3 (Fall 1994): 1–3.

6. Sally Miller Gearhart, "The Lesbian and God-the-Father, or All the Church Needs Is a Good Lay—on Its Side," *Radical Religion: Feminism and Religion* 1, no. 2 (Spring 1974).

7. Bernadette J. Brooten, *Love between Women: Early Christian Responses to Female Homoeroticism* (Chicago: Univ. of Chicago Press, 1996); Judith Plaskow, *The Coming of Lilith: Essays on Feminism, Judaism, and Sexual Ethics, 1972–2003* (Boston: Beacon, 2005); Carter Heyward, *Staying Power: Reflections on Gender, Justice, and Compassion* (Cleveland: Pilgrim, 1995); Virginia Ramey Mollenkott, *Sensuous Spirituality: Out from Fundamentalism* (New York: Crossroad, 1992); Mary E. Hunt, *Fierce Tenderness: A Feminist Theology of Friendship* (New York: Crossroad, 1991).

8. Traci C. West, *Sounds of the Spirit: Black Women, Violence, and Resistance Ethics* (New York: New York Univ. Press, 1999); Kelly Brown Douglas, *Sexuality and the Black Church: A Womanist Perspective* (Maryknoll, NY: Orbis Books, 1999).

9. Kwok Pui Lan, "Gay Activism in Asian and Asian-American Churches," http://thewitness.org/agw/kwok051904.html.

10. Virginia Ramey Mollenkott, *Omnigender: A Trans-religious Approach* (Cleveland: Pilgrim, 2001).

Chapter 6: Muslim Feminism and Islamic Reformation

1. For the studies on the interplay between Islam and other social institutions, see, for example, Yvonne Yazbcek Haddad and John L. Esposito, eds., *Islam, Gender, and Social Change* (New York: Oxford Univ. Press, 1998), and Deniz Kandiyoti, ed., *Women, Islam and the State* (Philadelphia: Temple Univ. Press, 1991).

2. *Jadid* means "new" in Arabic, Turkic, and Persian. The Jadid Movement and Tajdid derived from usul-i jadid (new methods) in teaching and school curricula used by jadidists in opposition to qadimists (old thinkers) in the maktab (school). Jadidism grew into a cultural reform, a nationalist modernist interpretation of Islam in Central Asia thanks to the endeavors of Muslim reformers such as the Crimean Tatar journalist Ismail Gasprinski.

3. See Mervat Hatem, "Secularist and Islamist Discourses on Modernity in Egypt and the Evolution of the Post-colonial Nation-State," and Afsaneh Najmabadi, "Feminism in an Islamic Republic: Years of Hardship, Years of Growth," in Haddad and Esposito, *Islam, Gender and Social Change*.

4. For such similarities and differences between Islamists of Iran and Afghanistan (the Taliban), see Mehrangiz Kar, "Women's Strategies in Iran from the 1979 Revolution to 1999," in *Globalization, Gender and Religion: The Politics of Women's Rights in Catholic and Muslim Contexts* ed. Jane Bayes and Nayereh Tohidi (New York: Palgrave, 2001), 177–203.

5. For a fascinating narration of such debates, see Ziba Mir-Hosseini, *Islam and Gender: The Religious Debate in Contemporary Iran* (Princeton, NJ: Princeton Univ. Press, 1999).

6. See the United Nations report in commemoration of the fiftieth anniversary of the Universal Declaration of Human Rights, December 1998; the Human Development Report of 1999 by the UNDP; and the 2000 Human Rights Watch World Report.

7. Belinda Clark, "The Vienna Convention Reservations Regime and the Convention on Discrimination against Women," *American Journal of International Law* 85 (1991): 317.

8. Ann Elizabeth Mayer, "Rhetorical Strategies and Official Policies on Women's Rights," in *Faith and Freedom: Women's Human Rights in the Muslim World*, ed. Mahnaz Afkhami (New York: I. B. Tauris, 1995), 104.

9. See Bayes and Tohidi, *Globalization, Gender, and Religion*, 2–6. Also see Colum Lynch, "Islamic Bloc, Christian Right Team Up to Lobby UN," *Washington Post*, June 17, 2002, A01.

10. See *Rouydad*, 19 Urdibehesht, 1382, or Iran-Emrooz, May 7, 2003 (http://www.iran-emrooz.de).

11. See http://www.zananiniran.com, Urdibehest 14, 1382/May 4, 2003.

12. See Mir-Hosseini, *Islam and Gender*, and "Mas'ale-ye zanan: Nov-andishi-ye dini ve feminism" (The Women Question: New Religious Thinking and Feminism), interview with Alireza Alavi-tabar, in the monthly *Aftab* 24 (Farvardin 1382/March 2003): 38–41.

13. Rough estimates based on three regions in Asia as reported in *The World's Women 2000: Trends and Statistics* (New York: United Nations Publications, 2000), 89, chart 4.5.

14. In the government offices, this rate is higher (31 percent) and in the informal sector much higher than the formal; see Maryam Poya, *Women, Work and Islamism: Ideology and Resistance in Iran* (London: Zed Books, 1999), 77–87.

15. Elsewhere, several scholars including myself have explained the reasons for the surge of Islamism and the significance of its gender dimension and the historical, geographic, economic, political, and cultural reasons for the extra strength and resistant nature of patriarchy in Iran and several other Muslim

societies. See, for instance, Nikki Keddie, "Women in Iran Since 1979," *Social Research* 67 (2002): 407–38; Kandiyoti 1991; Tohidi and Bayes, *Globalization, Gender and Religion*.

16. For information on this active Muslim feminist group, see http://www.sistersinislam.org.my.

17. Lila Abu-Lughod, ed., *Remaking Women: Feminism and Modernity in the Middle East* (Princeton, NJ: Princeton Univ. Press, 1998); Haleh Afshar, *Islam and Feminisms: An Iranian Case Study* (London: Macmillan, 1998); Leila Ahmed, *Women and Gender in Islam* (New Haven, CT: Yale Univ. Press, 1992); Aziza Al-Hibri, "Islam, Law and Custom: Redefining Muslim Women's Rights," *American University Journal of International Law and Policy* 12 (1997): 1–44; Margot Badran, "Toward Islamic Feminisms: A Look at the Middle East," in *Hermeneutics and Honor: Negotiating Female Public Space in Islamicate Societies*, ed. Asma Afsaruddin (Cambridge, MA: Harvard Univ. Press, 1999), 159–88; Asma Barlas, *"Believing Women" in Islam: Understanding Patriarchal Interpretations of the Quran* (Austin: Texas Univ. Press, 2002); Miriam Cooke, *Women Claiming Islam: Creating Islamic Feminism through Literature* (London: Routledge, 2000); Elizabeth W. Fernea, *In Search of Islamic Feminism* (New York: Doubleday, 1998); Erika Friedl, "Ideal Womanhood in Postrevolutionary Iran," in *Mixed Blessings: Gender and Religious Fundamentalism Cross-Culturally*, ed. Judy Brink and Joan Mencher (New York: Routledge, 1997); Azza Karam, *Women, Islamism, and State: Contemporary Feminism in Egypt* (London: Macmillan, 1998); Azadeh Kian-Thiebaut, "Women and Politics in Post-Islamist Iran," *British Journal of Middle Eastern Studies* 24 (1997): 75–96; Fatima Mernissi, *The Veil and the Male Elite: A Feminist Interpretation of Women's Rights in Islam*, trans. Mary Jo Lakeland (Reading, MA: Addison-Wesley, 1991); Ziba Mir-Hosseini, "Stretching the Limits: A Feminist Reading of Shari'a in Iran Today," in *Feminism and Islam: Legal and Literary Perspectives*, ed. Mai Yamani (New York: New York Univ. Press, 1996); Mir-Hosseini, *Islam and Gender*; Parvin Paidar, *Women and the Political Process in Twentieth-Century Iran* (Cambridge: Cambridge Univ. Press, 1995); Anne Sofie Roald, "Feminist Reinterpretation of Islamic Sources: Muslim Feminist Theology in the Light of the Christian Tradition of Feminist Thought," in *Women and Islamization: Contemporary Dimensions of Discourse on Gender Relations*, ed. Karin Ask and Marit Tjomsland (Oxford: Berg, 1998); Barbara F. Stowasser, *Women in the Qur'an, Traditions, and Interpretation* (New York: Oxford Univ. Press, 1994).

18. October 6, 2001, http://www.bbc.co.uk/persian/news/011006_vleader.shtml.

19. Ibid.

20. Omaima Abou-Bakr, "Islamic Feminism? What's in a Name?," *Middle East Women's Studies Review* (Winter–Spring 2001): 1–3.

21. Hoda El-Sadda, cited in ibid.

22. Author's interview with Shirin Ebadi, December 1999.

23. Ahmed, *Women and Gender in Islam*, 168.

24. http://www.bbc.co.uk/persian/news/011006_vleader.shtml.

25. See Bayes and Tohidi, *Globalization, Gender and Religion*.

26. See, for instance, Elisabeth Schüssler Fiorenza, *But She Said: Feminist Practices of Biblical Interpretation* (Boston: Beacon, 1992), and Rosemary Radford Ruether, "Christianity and Women in the Modern World," in *Today's Woman in World Religions*, ed. Arvind Sharma (Albany: State Univ. of New York Press, 1993).

27. Amina Wadud, *Qur'an and Woman: Rereading the Sacred Text from a Woman's Perspective* (New York: Oxford Univ. Press, 1999).

28. See Barbara F. Stowasser, "Gender Issues and Contemporary Quran Interpretation," in Haddad and Esposito, *Islam, Gender and Social Change*.

29. Azizah Al-Hibri, "Islam, Law, and Custom: Redefining Muslim Women's Rights," *American University Journal of International Law and Policy* 12 (1997): 2.

30. Ibid.

31. Roald, "Feminist Reinterpretation of Islamic Sources," 41.

32. Mir-Hosseini, *Islam and Gender*.

33. Friedl, "Ideal Womanhood in Postrevolutionary Iran," 146.

34. For the significant contributions of Saeedzadeh (some of which appeared under female pseudonyms), see Mir-Hosseini, *Islam and Gender*, and Kar, "Women's Strategies in Iran from the 1979 Revolution to 1999."

35. See "Mas'ale-ye zanan: Nov andishi-ye dini ve feminism," 39.

36. Ibid., 40.

37. Ibid., 41.

38. Vahdat, Farzin. *God and Juggernaut: Iran's Intellectual Encounter with Modernity* (Syracuse: Syracuse UP, 2002).

Chapter 7: Buddhist Feminist Scholars

1. Caroline Rhys Davids, *The Psalms of the Early Buddhists, Vol. I: Psalms of the Sisters* (London: published for the Pali Text Society by Henry Frowde, Oxford Univ. Press warehouse, Amen Corner, E.C., 1909).

2. Ibid., 15.

3. Ibid., 29.

4. The books of the Buddhist canon were transcribed from the oral teachings into two different languages, Sanskrit and Pali, a ceremonial language similar to Sanskrit but having its own distinct quality.

5. I. B. Horner, *Women under Primitive Buddhism* (Delhi: Motilal Banarsidass, 1975 [1930]).

6. Of course, in Buddhist thought we understand that the gender identities of man and woman are no more than ever-changing forms in the world of conditioned existence, that they have no solidity and no real existence, that liberation lies beyond all distinctions and opposites. This is what is called "emptiness." But while understanding this and experiencing it during some of our practice, we also live in the world of forms and must work with them, holding both with equal attention. The Heart Sutra tells us, "Form does not differ from emptiness, emptiness does not differ from form."

7. Rhys Davids, *Psalms of the Sisters*, 78.

8. Diana Paul, *Women in Buddhism: Images of the Feminine in Mahayana Tradition* (Berkeley: Asian Humanities Press, 1979).

9. Ibid., 41 (both verses).

10. Tsultrim Allione, *Women of Wisdom* (London: Routledge & Kegan Paul, 1984).

11. Rick Fields, *How the Swans Came to the Lake* (Boulder, CO: Shambhala, 1981).

12. Sandy Boucher, *Turning the Wheel: American Women Creating the New Buddhism* (Boston: Beacon, 1993 [1988]).

13. Karma Lekse Tsomo, *Sakyadhita: Daughters of the Buddha* (Ithaca, NY: Snow Lion, 1988).

14. Rita Gross, *Buddhism after Patriarchy: A Feminist History, Analysis and Reconstruction of Buddhism* (Albany: State Univ. of New York Press, 1993).

15. Miranda Shaw, *Passionate Enlightenment: Women in Tantric Buddhism* (Princeton: Princeton UP, 1994).

16. Anne Klein, *Meeting the Great Bliss Queen: Buddhists, Feminists, and the Art of the Self* (Boston: Beacon, 1995).

17. Judith Simmer-Brown, *Dakini's Warm Breath: The Feminine Principle in Tibetan Buddhism* (Boston: Shambhala, 2001).

Chapter 8: Women, Religion, and the Ecological Crisis

1. Division of Early Warning and Assessment, United Nations Environment Programme, *Millennium Ecosystem Assessment* (2005).

2. Harvard University Center for the Environment: http://environ-ment.harvard.edu/religion.

3. Hava Tirosh-Samuelson, ed., *Judaism and Ecology: Created World and Revealed Word*, Religions of the World and Ecology (Cambridge, MA: Harvard Univ. Press, 2002).

4. Ellen Bernstein, *The Splendor of Creation: A Biblical Ecology* (Cleveland: Pilgrim, 2005).

5. Paul Ehrlich and Donald Kennedy, "Millennium Assessment of Human Behavior," *Science* 309 (July 22, 2005): 562–63.

6. Mihaly Csikszentmihalyi, *The Evolving Self: A Psychology for the Third Millennium* (New York: HarperCollins, 1993), 19.

Chapter 9: Prayer as Poetry, Poetry as Prayer

1. All poems and blessings cited in this chapter are from Marcia Falk, *The Book of Blessings: New Jewish Prayers for Daily Life, the Sabbath, and the New Moon Festival* (San Francisco: Harper, 1996; paperback, New York: Beacon, 1999), and are used by permission.

Select Bibliography

Rosemary Radford Ruether, Writing on Women

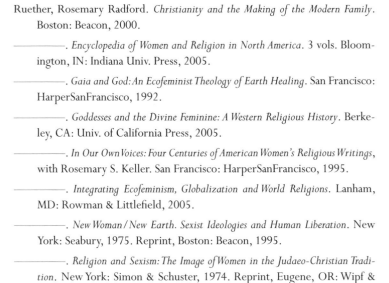

Ruether, Rosemary Radford. *Christianity and the Making of the Modern Family*. Boston: Beacon, 2000.

——. *Encyclopedia of Women and Religion in North America*. 3 vols. Bloomington, IN: Indiana Univ. Press, 2005.

——. *Gaia and God: An Ecofeminist Theology of Earth Healing*. San Francisco: HarperSanFrancisco, 1992.

——. *Goddesses and the Divine Feminine: A Western Religious History*. Berkeley, CA: Univ. of California Press, 2005.

——. *In Our Own Voices: Four Centuries of American Women's Religious Writings*, with Rosemary S. Keller. San Francisco: HarperSanFrancisco, 1995.

——. *Integrating Ecofeminism, Globalization and World Religions*. Lanham, MD: Rowman & Littlefield, 2005.

——. *New Woman / New Earth. Sexist Ideologies and Human Liberation*. New York: Seabury, 1975. Reprint, Boston: Beacon, 1995.

——. *Religion and Sexism: The Image of Women in the Judaeo-Christian Tradition*. New York: Simon & Schuster, 1974. Reprint, Eugene, OR: Wipf & Stock, 1998.

—————. *Sexism and God-Talk: Toward a Feminist Theology*. Boston: Beacon, 1963. Reprint, Boston: Beacon, 1993.

—————. *Women and Redemption: A Theological History*. Minneapolis: Fortress Press, 1998.

—————. *Women and Religion in America: 1900–1968: A Documentary History*, with Rosemary S. Keller. New York: Harper & Row, 1986.

—————. *Women and Religion in America: The Colonial and Revolutionary War Periods, A Documentary History*, with Rosemary S. Keller. New York: Harper & Row, 1983.

—————. *Women-Church: Theology and Practice of Feminist Liturgical Communities*. New York: Harper & Row, 1986.

—————. *Women-Guides: Texts for Feminist Theology*. Boston: Beacon, 1986. Reprint, Boston: Beacon, 1995.

—————. *Women Healing Earth: Third World Women on Feminism, Religion and Ecology*. Maryknoll, NY: Orbis Books, 1996.

—————. *Women of Spirit: Female Leadership in the Jewish and Christian Traditions*, with Eleanor McLaughlin. New York: Simon & Schuster, 1978. Reprint, Wipf & Stock, 1998.

Peggy H. Cleveland, Reflections on the Early Years

Bennett, Anne McGrew. *From Woman Pain to Woman Vision: Writings in Feminist Theology*, edited by Mary Hunt. Minneapolis: Fortress Press, 1989.

Bunch, Charlotte. *Passionate Politics: Essays 1968–1986: Feminist Theory in Action*. New York: St. Martin's Press, 1990.

Harrison, Beverly. *Our Right to Choose: Toward a New Ethics of Abortion*. Boston: Beacon, 1983.

—————. *Making the Connections: Essays in Feminist Social Ethics*. Boston: Beacon, 1985.

Jarl, Ann-Cathrin. *Justice, Women and Global Economics*. Minneapolis: Fortress Press, 2003.

Klein, Kim. *Fundraising for Social Change*. Inverness, CA: Chardon Press, 1988.

Morton, Nelle. *The Journey Is Home*. Boston: Beacon, 1985.

Waugh, Barbara. *Soul in the Computer: The Story of a Corporate Revolutionary*. Makawao, Maui: Inner Ocean, 2001.

Wire, Antoinette Clark. *The Corinthian Women Prophets: A Reconstruction through Paul's Rhetoric*. Minneapolis: Fortress Press, 1990.

Pamela Cooper-White, The Early 1990s

Chinnici, Rosemary. *Can Women Re-image the Church?*. New York: Paulist Press, 1992.

Cooper-White, Pamela. *The Cry of Tamar: Violence against Women and the Church's Response*. Minneapolis: Fortress Press, 1995.

——. *Shared Wisdom: The Use of the Self in Pastoral Care and Counseling*. Minneapolis: Fortress Press, 2004.

DeMarinis, Valerie. *Critical Caring: A Feminist Model for Pastoral Psychotherapy*. Louisville: Westminster John Knox, 1994.

Hooks, Bell. *Feminist Theory: From Margin to Center*. Boston: South End, 1984.

Jordan, Judith, et al. *Growth in Connection: Writings from the Stone Center*. New York: Guilford, 1991.

Klein, Melanie. *Envy and Gratitude and Other Works, 1946–1963*. New York: Free Press, 1984.

Miller, Jean Baker. *Toward a New Psychology of Women*. 2nd edition. Boston: Beacon, 1987.

Rhodes, Lynn. *Co-creating: A Feminist Vision of Ministry*. Louisville: Westminster John Knox, 1987.

Spahr, Jane, Kathryn Poethig, and Melinda McLain, eds. *Called Out: The Voice and Gifts of Lesbian, Gay, Bisexual and Transgendered Presbyerians*. Gathersburg, MD: Chi Rho, 1995.

Stortz, Martha Elle. *PastorPower*. Nashville: Abingdon, 1991.

Cheryl Kirk-Duggan, Dreams, Visions, and Disconnects

Kirk-Duggan, Cheryl. *Exorcising Evil: A Womanist Perspective on the Spirituals*. Maryknoll, NY: Orbis Books, 1997.

——. *Misbegotten Anguish: A Theology and Ethics of Violence*. St. Louis, MO: Chalice Press, 2001.

——. *Pregnant Passion: Gender, Sex and Violence in the Bible*. Atlanta: Society of Biblical Literature, 2003.

——. *Refiner's Fire: A Religious Engagement with Violence*. Minneapolis: Fortress Press, 2001.

——. *Soul Pearls: Worship Resources for the Black Church*. Nashville: Abingdon, 2003.

Rita Nakashima Brock,
Feminism and Asian American Women

Brock, Rita Nakashima. *Journeys by Heart: A Christology of Erotic Power*. New York: Crossroads, 1988.

Brock, Rita Nakashima, and Rebecca Parker. *Proverbs of Ashes: Violence, Redemptive Suffering and the Search for What Saves Us*. Boston: Beacon, 2001.

Brock, Rita Nakashima, and Susan Thistlethwaite. *Casting Stones: Prostitution and Liberation in Asia and the United States*. Minneapolis: Fortress Press, 1996.

—————. *Saving Paradise*. Boston: Beacon, 2007.

Kim, Grace Ji-Sun. *The Grace of Sophia: A Korean North America Women's Christology*. Cleveland: Pilgrim, 2000.

Kwok Pui Lan. *Discovering the Bible in the Non-Biblical World. Maryknoll*. NY: Orbis Books, 1995.

—————. *Introducing Asian Feminist Theology*. Cleveland: Pilgrim, 2000.

Nancy Pineda Madrid, Hispanic American Feminism

Alarcón, Norma. "Chicana Feminist Literature." In *This Bridge Called My Back: Writings by Radical Women of Color*. Edited by Cherrie Moraga and Gloria Anzalua. New York: Kitchen Table: Women of Color Press, 1983, 182–190.

Anzaldua, Gloria. *Borderlands/La Frontera: The New Mestiza*. San Francisco: Spinsters/Aunt Lute, 1987.

Aquino, Maria Pilar. *Our Cry for Life: Feminist Theology from Latin America*. Maryknoll, NY: Orbis Books, 1993.

Gonzalez, Michelle. *Sor Juana: Beauty and Justice in the Americas*. Maryknoll, NY: Orbis Books, 2003.

Isasi-Díaz, Ada María. *En La Lucha: A Hispanic Women's Liberation Theology*. Minneapolis: Fortress Press, 1993.

—————. *La Lucha Continues: Mujerista Theology*. Maryknoll, NY: Orbis Books, 2004.

—————. *Mujerista Theology*. Maryknoll, NY: Orbis Books, 1996.

Isasi-Díaz, Ada María, and Yolana Tarango. *Hispanic Women, Prophetic Voice in the Church; Toward a Hispanic Women's Liberation Theology*. San Francisco: Harper & Row, 1988.

Madrid, Nancy Pineda. "In Search of a Theology of Suffering Latinamente." In *Ties That Bind: African-American and Hispanic-American/Latino Theology in the United States*. Edited by Antony Pinn and Benjamin Valentin. New York: Continuum, 2001, 184–99.

————. "Chicano Feminist Epistemology." In *A Reader in Latina Feminist Theology:Religion and Justice.* Edited by Maria Pilar Aquino, Daisy Machado, and Jeanette Rodriguez. Austin: Univ. of Texas Press, 2002, 241–66.

Stephanie Y. Mitchem, Womanist Theology

Cannon, Katie G. *Katie's Canon: Womanism and the Soul of the Black Community.* New York: Continuum, 1995.

Douglas, Kelly Brown. *The Black Christ.* Maryknoll, NY: Orbis Books, 1994.

————. *Sexuality and the Black Church: A Womanist Perspective.* Maryknoll, NY: Orbis Books, 1999.

Giddings, Paula. *When and Where I Enter: The Impact of Black Women on Race and Sex in America.* New York: Bantam, 1984.

Hall, Gloria T, Patricia Bell-Scott, and Barbara Smith. *All the Women Were White, All the Blacks Were Men, and Some of Us Were Brave.* Old Westbury, NY: Feminist Press, 1982.

Martin, Joan M. *More Than Chains and Toil: A Christian Work Ethics of Enslaved Black Women.* Louisville: Westminster John Knox, 2000.

Mitchem, Stephanie Y. *Introducing Womanist Theology.* Maryknoll, NY: Orbis Books, 2002.

————. *African-American Women Tapping Power and Spiritual Wellness.* Cleveland: Pilgrim Press, 2004.

Riggs, Maria. *Awake, Arise and Act: A Womanist Call for Liberation.* Cleveland: Pilgrim, 1994.

————. *Plenty Good Room: Women Versus Male Power in the Black Church.* Cleveland: Pilgrim, 2003.

Townes, Emilie. *Breaking the Fine Rain of Death: African-American Health Issues and a Womanist Ethic of Care.* New York: Continuum, 1998.

————. *Embracing the Spirit: Womanist Perspectives on Hope, Salvation and Transformation.* Maryknoll, NY: Orbis Books, 199.

————. *In a Blaze of Glory: Womanist Spirituality as Social Witness.* Nashville: Abingdon, 1995.

————. *A Troubling in My Soul: Womanist Perspectives on Evil and Suffering.* Maryknoll, NY: Orbis Books, 1993.

————. *Womanist Justice, Womanist Hope.* Atlanta: Scholars Press, 1993.

Walker, Alice. *In Search of Our Mothers' Gardens.* San Diego: Harcourt Brace & Jovanovich, 1983.

Mary E. Hunt, Lesbian Perspectives on Feminist Theology

Brooten, Bernadette J. *Love between Women: Early Christian Responses to Female Homoeroticism*. Chicago: Univ. of Chicago Press, 1996.

Heyward, Carter. *Our Passion for Justice: Images of Power, Sexuality and Liberation*. New York: Pilgrim, 1989.

——. *Staying Power: Reflections on Gender, Justice and Compassion*. Cleveland: Pilgrim, 1995.

Hunt, Mary E. *Fierce Tenderness: A Feminist Theology of Friendship*. New York: Crossroads, 1991.

——. *Good Sex*. With Patricia B. Jung and Radhika Balakrishnan. New Brunswick, NJ: Rutgers Univ. Press, 2001.

——. *A Guide to Women in Religion: Making Your Way from A to Z*. New York: Palgrave Macmillan, 2004.

Mollencott, Virginia Ramey. *Sensuous Spirituality: Out from Fundamentalism*. New York: Crossroads, 1992.

——. *Omnigender: A Transreligous Approach*. Cleveland: Pilgrim, 2001.

Plaskow, Judith. *The Coming of Lilith: Essays on Feminism, Judaism and Sexual Ethics, 1972–2003*. Boston: Beacon, 2005.

Nayereh Tohidi, Women and Islam

Abu-Lughod, Lila, ed. *Remaking Women: Feminism and Modernity in the Middle East*. Princeton: Princeton Univ. Press, 1998.

Afkhami, Mahnaz. *Faith and Freedom: Women's Human Rights in the Muslim World*. New York: I. B. Tauris, 1995.

Afsaruddin, Asma, ed. *Hermeneutics and Honor: Negotiating Female Public Space in Islamicate Societies*. Cambridge, MA: Harvard Univ. Press, 1999.

Ahmad, Leila. *Women and Gender in Islam*. New Haven, CT: Yale Univ. Press, 1992.

Ansari, Sarah, and Vanessa Martin. *Women, Religion and Culture in Iran*. London: Curzon, 2002.

Ask, Karin, and Marit Tjomstand. *Women and Islamization: Contemporary Dimensions of Discourse on Gender Relations*. Oxford: Berg, 1998.

Barlas, Asma. *"Believing Women" in Islam: Understanding Patriarchal Interpretations of the Quran*. Austin: Texas Univ. Press, 2002.

Cooke, Miriam. *Women Claiming Islam: Creating Islamic Feminism through Literature*. London: Routledge, 2000.

Fernea, Elizabeth. *In Search of Islamic Feminism*. New York: Doubleday, 1998.

Haddad, Yvonne Y., and John L. Esposito, eds. *Islam, Feminism and Social Change*. New York: Oxford Univ. Press, 1998.

Kamalkhomi, Zahira. *Women's Islam: Religious Practice among Women in Today's Iran*. London: Kegan Paul, 1998.

Karam, Azza. *Women, Islamism and State: Contemporary Feminism in Egypt*. London: Macmillan, 1998.

Keddie, Nikki R. *Debating Gender, Debating Sexuality*. New York: New York UP, 1996.

Keddie, Nikki R., and Beth Baron. *Women in Middle East History: Shifting Boundaries in Sex and Gender*. New Haven, CT: Yale Univ. Press, 1992.

Keddie, Nikki R., and Lois Beck. *Women in the Muslim World*, Cambridge: Harvard Univ. Press, 1978.

Mirnissi, Fatima. *Beyond the Veil: Male-Female Dynamics in a Modern Muslim Society*. Cambridge, MA: Schenknam, 1975.

—————. *The Veil and the Male Elite: A Feminist Interpretation of Women's Rights in Islam*. Cambridge, MA: Perseus Books, 1991.

Mir-Hosseini, Ziba. *Islam and Gender: The Religious Debate in Contemporary Iran*. Princeton: Princeton Univ. Press, 1999.

Paidar, Parvin. *Women and the Political Process in Twentieth Century Iran*. Cambridge, England; New York: Cambridge Univ. Press, 1995.

Tabari, Azar, and Nahid Yeganeh. *In the Shadow of Islam*. London: Zed Books, 1982.

Tohidi, Nayereh. *Feminism, Democracy and Islamism in Iran*. Los Angeles: Ketabsara, 1996.

Tohidi, Nayereh, and Herbert Bodman. *Women in Muslim Societies: Diversity within Unity*. Boulder: Lynne Rienner, 1998.

Tohidi, Nayereh, and Jane Bayes, eds. *Globalization, Gender and Religion: The Politics of Women's Rights in Catholic and Muslim Contexts*. New York: Palgrave, 2001.

Stowasser, Barbara F. *Women in the Quran: Tradition and Interpretation*. New York: Oxford Univ. Press, 1994.

Yamani, Mai, ed. *Feminism and Islam: Legal and Literary Perspectives*. New York: New York Univ. Press, 1996.

Wadud, Amina. *Quran and Women: Rereading Sacred Text from a Woman's Perspective*. Oxford, England; New York: Oxford Univ. Press, 1999.

Sandy Boucher, Buddhism and Women

Allione, Tsaltrim. *Women of Wisdom*. London: Routledge & Kegan Paul, 1984.

Boucher, Sandy. *Turning the Wheel: American Women Creating the New Buddhism*. San Francisco: Harper & Row, 1988. Reprint, Boston: Beacon, 1993.

Gross, Rita. *Buddhism after Patriarchy: A Feminist History, Analysis and Reconstruction of Buddhism*. Albany, NY: SUNY Press, 1993.

——. *Soaring and Settling: Buddhist Perspectives on Contemporary Social and Religious Issues*. New York: Continuum, 1998.

Horner, Isaline Blew. *Women under Primitive Buddhism*. Delhi: Motilal Barnarsides, 1930. Reprint, 1975.

Klein, Anne. *Meeting the Great Bliss Queen: Buddhists, Feminists and the Art of the Self*. Boston: Beacon, 1995.

Paul, Diana. *Women in Buddhism: Image of the Feminine in Mahayana Tradition*. Berkeley: Asian Humanities Press, 1979.

Shaw, Miranda. *Passionate Enlightenment: Women in Tantric Buddhism*. Princeton: Princeton Univ. Press, 1994.

Simmer-Brown, Judith. *Dakini's Warm Breath: The Feminine Principle in Tibetan Buddhism*. Boston: Shambhala Publishing, 2001.

Tsome, Karma Lekse Tsome. *Sakyadhilta: Daughters of the Buddha*. Ithaca: Snow Lion, 1988.

Mary Evelyn Tucker, Ecology and World Religions

Tucker, Mary Evelyn. *Worldly Wonder: Religions Enter Their Ecological Phase*. Chicago: Open Court Press, 2003.

Tucker, Mary Evelyn, and John Berthrong. *Confucianism and Ecology: The Interrelation of Heaven, Earth and Humans*. Cambridge, MA: Harvard Univ. Press, 1998.

Tucker, Mary Evelyn, and Christopher Key Chapple. *Hinduism and Ecology: The Intersection of Earth, Sky and Water*. Cambridge, MA: Harvard Univ. Press, 2000.

Tucker, Mary Evelyn, and John Grim. *World Views and Ecology: Religion, Philosophy and Environment*. Maryknoll, NY: Orbis Books, 1994.

Tucker, Mary Evelyn, Clifford N. Matthews, and Philip Hefner. *When Worlds Converge: What Science and Religion Tell Us about the Universe Story*. Chicago: Open Court Press, 2002.

Tucker, Mary Evelyn, and Tu Weiming. *Confucian Spirituality*. New York: Crossroads, 2003.

Tucker, Mary Evelyn, and Duncan Ryuken Williams. *Buddhism and Ecology: The Interconnection of Dharma and Deeds*. Cambridge, MA: Harvard Univ. Press, 1997.

Marcia Falk: Jewish Feminist Theology

Adler, Rachel. *Engendering Judaism: An Inclusive Theology and Ethics*. Philadelphia: Jewish Publishing Society, 1998.

Falk, Marcia. *The Book of Blessings: New Jewish Prayers for Daily Life, the Sabbath, and the New Moon Festival*. San Francisco: Harper, 1996; Boston: Beacon Press, 1999.

——————. *The Song of Songs: Love Lyrics from the Bible*. Hanover and London: Brandeis Univ. Press/Univ. Press of New England, 2004.

Falk, Marcia, trans. *The Spectacular Difference: Selected Poems of Zelda*. Cincinnati: Hebrew Union College Press, 2004.

——————. *With Teeth in the Earth: Selected Poems of Malka Heifetz Tussman*. Detroit: Wayne State Univ. Press, 1992.

Gottlieb, Lynn. *She Who Dwells Within: A Feminist Vision of Renewed Judaism*. New York: HarperCollins, 1995.

Heschel, Susannah, ed. *On Being a Jewish Feminist: A Reader*. New York: Schocken, 1983.

Plaskow, Judith. *Standing Again at Sinai: Judaism from a Feminist Perspective*. New York: Harper & Row, 1990.

Umansky, Ellen M., and Dianne Ashton, eds. *Four Centuries of Jewish Women's Spirituality: A Sourcebook*. Boston: Beacon Press, 1992.